Formalism & Intuition in Software Development

Michael A. Jackson
Edgar G. Daylight

A conversation with Michael A. Jackson
conducted by Edgar G. Daylight and Bas van Vlijmen
on March 8th, 2013 in Amsterdam, the Netherlands,
and by Edgar G. Daylight on July 22nd, 2013 in London, England.
Edited by Kurt De Grave.

LONELY SCHOLAR™
SCIENTIFIC BOOKS

Conversations issue 5
First edition
Version 1.0
This issue is exceptionally in British English.

© 2015 Edgar G. Daylight
Cover design © 2015 Kurt De Grave
Back cover photo © 2013 Edgar G. Daylight

Daylight can be contacted at egdaylight@dijkstrascry.com.

Published by Lonely Scholar bvba
Dr. Van De Perrestraat 127
2440 Geel
Belgium
http://www.lonelyscholar.com

Typeset in LaTeX

D/2015/12.695/1
ISBN 978-94-91386-05-3
ISSN 2034-5976
NUR 980, 686

Contents

1   Childhood & University   4

2   Jackson Structured Programming   11

3   Working Group 2.3   30

4   Program Transformation Systems   39

5   Dijkstra's Pleasantness Problem   47

6   Countering Top-Down Design   54

7   Jackson System Development   60

8   AT&T   71

9   Problem Frames   77

10 Past, Future, and Adjacent Fields   83

Bibliography   89

Index   94

Preface

Software technology can be viewed through very different lenses. The words 'computer program', for instance, have acquired at least four different meanings during the course of history. A computer program can refer to:

1. a technological object,

2. a mathematical object of finite capacity,

3. a mathematical object of infinite size, or

4. a model of the real world, which is not a logico-mathematical construction.

Proponents of the fourth viewpoint oppose a rational metaphysical view to our digital world. They state that not every 'computer program' can be understood by resorting solely to logic and strict rules. James Moor, for instance, wrote in 1978 that computer scientists have an inclination to slide, in their discourse, between programs, models, and theories as if there was no distinction between them [43] and the philosopher Hubert Dreyfus scrutinized the entire field of Artificial Intelligence in his 1972 book *What Computers Can't Do* [17]. More names in this regard are James Fetzer [19], Peter Naur [10], and Brian Cantwell Smith [53].

Michael A. Jackson's views align well with those of the aforementioned actors. During the 1960s and 1970s, Jackson came to view a data processing system as a simulation of the real world and in subsequent decades he pondered and published about the difference between the little, 'well formalizable', math problems of Edsger Dijkstra and cyber-physical systems, which have requirements that are 'possibly completely infeasible to formalize'. In the conversation that follows, Jackson describes the 1970s as a decade that gave way to formal mathematical concerns, leading to a widening split between academia and industry. The role of mathematics in software engineering, Jackson says today, should be 'as the servant, rather than queen, of the sciences'.

It is in the field of data processing that Jackson began his computing career, encountering a computer for the first time in 1961. After starting his company Michael Jackson Systems Ltd. in 1971, he developed the Jackson structured programming (JSP) design method and later elaborated that into Jackson system development (JSD). During these years, he began to realize that different software development problems demand different methodologies. His research papers of the 1980s and onwards reveal a deep fascination for the fundamental question: What is software engineering? In the present booklet Jackson also repeatedly reflects on the constituents of software development; he compares and contrasts the writings of several contemporaries, including Ole-Johan Dahl, Edsger Dijkstra, Barry Dwyer, Tony Hoare, Donald Knuth, Pierre-Arnoul de Marneffe, Peter Naur, Brian Randell, Christopher Strachey, David Parnas, and Pamela Zave. Some of the many interrelated topics that come to the fore are software malleability, program transformation systems, and the history of automobile engineering.

The present booklet is the result of two 'oral history' interviews with Jackson. The first was conducted by Bas van Vlijmen and myself on 8 March 2013 in Amsterdam. The second interview was held on 22 July 2013 in Jackson's house in London, where he and I discussed the past for an entire day. I transcribed the interviews and Jackson re-wrote and refined several parts of the transcript. The polished and insightful text that follows is the product of an authentic software scholar who, as he told me when I left his house, 'feels so lucky to have experienced the beginnings of our digital world'. The history of computing is very fortunate to have him share his reflections and insights with us here.

— Edgar G. Daylight, 15 February 2015, Geel, Belgium

Short Biography

Michael Jackson was born in 1936 in England. He obtained degrees in classics (Oxford) and mathematics (Cambridge). In 1961, he began his computing career in consultancy: first at Maxwell Stamp Associates, and then at John Hoskyns & Co. During the 1960s, his first ideas on program design were developed in cooperation with Barry Dwyer. Having started his company Michael Jackson Systems Ltd. in 1971, he then developed these ideas into the JSP program design method and later, in cooperation with John Cameron, into the system development method JSD. From 1990 he worked as an independent consultant, writer, and researcher, and also worked part-time with Pamela Zave at Bell Telephone Laboratories and AT&T Research. He has held visiting posts at the University of Strathclyde, UMIST, the University of Manchester, the University of Newcastle, and Imperial College. Since 2001 he has been a visiting professor at The Open University. Since 1973 he has been a member of the IFIP Working Group 2.3 on Programming Methodology; in 1995 he was a founding member of the IFIP Working Group 2.9 on Requirements Engineering. He has received the Stevens Award (1997), the Lovelace Medal of the British Computer Society (1998), the IEEE Achievement Medal (1998), and the ACM SIGSOFT Outstanding Research Award (2001).

1. Childhood & University

Daylight: What was your childhood like?

Jackson: I was born in England in 1936. I had a mother, a father, and an older sister. Our family home has been in London since I was two years old. During the Second World War we travelled quite a lot to avoid the bombing in London. My mother took my sister and me to stay with her family in Scotland, in Glasgow, Edinburgh, and Ayr. We also lived for some months in Gloucestershire: in Newent, Cheltenham, and elsewhere. We were not a very intellectual family, but my parents wanted my sister and me to have a good education. So when we returned to live in London after the war I went to a preparatory school, then to a good English public school where Christopher Strachey was teaching mathematics, and then on to university.

D: What do you remember from the war?

J: In Britain there was a threat of an invasion in 1940 but it never happened. A national government had been formed in that year with politicians from the main political parties. The government established a rationing scheme: initially for food, but later for clothes and other things as well. The food rationing was very stringent. Every week you got two ounces of butter, eight ounces of meat or something like that. We had a ration book with little coupons. When you went to the shop, when you bought the food you tore off the coupons and give them to the shopkeeper. The Labour Government of 1945 to 1950 continued food rationing: the effect was that the British population was healthier in the years from 1940 to 1950 than it has ever been before or since. Because I was a child—I was three and a half years old when the war broke out in 1939—I had no recollection of the days when you could have as much cream or meat as you wanted, when you could make a 12-egg omelette. So rationing never seemed a hardship to me, although it must have been difficult for adults.

One reason for additional limitations on food supply was the scarcity of imported food. The Germans were trying to impose an embargo, especially in the North Atlantic where their submarines attacked merchant ships. It became impossible to import fruit that did not grow in Britain. You could get such fruit only if you knew somebody in the navy who came home from a voyage bringing a few bananas, a couple of oranges, or something like that. Of course there was a black market and some people did manage to get such things; but for most people and certainly for our family there was no way at all. But like other children of my age I had never eaten them and so I did not miss them.

That's what my life was. I do remember one scarcity which I was aware of in a childish way. Do you know what Meccano was?

D: I was waiting for you to mention Meccano. Many people whom I have interviewed, including Niklaus Wirth [11, p.107], have mentioned Meccano when discussing their childhood. But I don't know a lot about it myself.

J: It was a construction set of mechanical parts. It was extremely good. It had gear wheels, pinions, bevel gears, axles, couplings, pivots, girders, strips, plates, bolts, nuts, and hundreds of other parts. You could make wonderful things with it. People made clocks, gearboxes, all sorts of things. When I was five—that must have been in 1941—my parents gave me a Number 5 Meccano set as a birthday present. In 1942 I got a 5A, which made it into a Number 6. The pinnacle of ambition in Meccano in those years was to possess the largest set, a Number 10. But after the 5A there were no more presents. The Meccano factory had been required by the government to make some kind of munitions for the war effort. So there were no more Meccano sets. This affected me deeply. I used to say to myself every night: 'I hope that by the time I'm ten, I can get a Number 10 Meccano set'. I didn't; but I did get one when I was 13 years old. I succeeded in making an automatic gearbox, and I was very happy with that.

That was the only sense in which I felt any deprivation at all. Compared to life in occupied Western Europe or in the battlefields of Eastern Europe it was absolutely nothing. There was the bombing of course. I was too young to know about the London blitz of 1940 and 1941, and we were mostly away from London in those years. But I was older in 1944 and 1945 and I remember the V1 flying bombs and the V2 rockets. There were two kinds of air raid shelter you could have. One was called a Morrison shelter, which was a big steel table with girders at the corners and wire mesh around it. We had a Morrison shelter in our living room and at night my sister and I slept there. The belief was that even if the house fell down, you would be safe in the Morrison shelter because the top would protect you from falling masonry. But there was also another kind of shelter, called the Anderson shelter, which was a dug out in your back garden with brick reinforcement. Our neighbours had an Anderson shelter. I remember going down into their Anderson shelter and sitting there hearing the sound of the V1. It had an engine which cut out. When you heard the engine cut out, you knew it was going to come down. So everyone said that if you heard the bang you were safe: the bomb hadn't landed on you. For me this was childish fun and excitement. My parents must have been terrified, but I wasn't: I was a child, pleased to be out of bed and drinking cocoa in the middle of the night.

D: Did you have any hobbies other than playing with your Meccano set? Horse riding perhaps?

J: Not really that I remember. I was a very limited child. Of course I still am a very limited child. I liked reading but essentially it was children's reading. When I started going to school more seriously, at the age of about eight, I became interested in various things, especially mathematics. I was quite successful in a number of school subjects but not in a serious way. I liked reading about the technology of the time and about earlier inventions. I remember a fine book, *Inventors' Cavalcade*, by Egon Larsen. He described great inventors—James Watt, Alexander Graham Bell, Thomas Alva Edison, Guglielmo Marconi, and others—and explained their inventions. I still have my copy.

D: How did you meet Christopher Strachey?

J: He was a schoolmaster at Harrow for a couple of years, where I was a pupil. Because of the slightly crazy education system, which was always changing in England, I had to decide at the age of 13 or 14 whether to go into the classical lower fifth form or the mathematical lower fifth. I knew that I was going to be a barrister, a lawyer. And I knew that barristers needed a fluent command of Latin. On that basis I chose the classical lower fifth. I did not become a barrister. Barristers don't need a fluent command of Latin. And what I ended up doing didn't really exist when I made that decision. That must have been in 1949.

When I was in the classical lower fifth, I and the other pupils of my year sat the School Certificate examination in many subjects. A regulation was in force—for quite short duration, I think—that you couldn't earn your certificate officially, except by taking the examination at the age of 16. But my friends and I were too young. Nevertheless, when we entered the classical upper fifth, we stopped formal lessons in mathematics, French, history, geography—almost everything. It was rather ridiculous. We knew that in two years time we would have to sit the School Certificate examination again in many subjects. So there was an attempt to keep us interested enough to remember something of what we had learned and to sit the exam.

One part of that was a little light mathematics, taught by Christopher Strachey who was a maths teacher at the school. He told us about Cantor's enumeration of rationals, the cardinalities of infinite sets, Klein bottles, Möbius strips, and other exciting—almost recreational—pieces of mathematics.

At the time, Strachey was living at the school, just outside London, and writing programs, first for the Pilot ACE and then for the Manchester Mark I. His program to play draughts—checkers—became very well known. He thought that programming was something that would interest us as part of our mathematical education.

Looking back, what he did was invent a little language for handling small integers with assignment, equality tests, a jump, and so on. We then set about writing programs for doing things like multiplication, division, and so on. I thought this was really marvellous. I remember he showed me his draughts-playing program which he had written out in pencil in machine code. I recollect a sheet of paper, the program written in two columns with lines showing where the jumps went. He told me something about the program, including an error he had made. If the opponent was about to promote a piece to a king, his program preferred to sacrifice one of its own pieces to any other move. He delighted in pointing out that this was an error in his specification, not in his programming. This must have been in 1950 or 1951. He took the class on an outing to the Festival of Britain, where I remember seeing a machine that played the game of Nim, and being inspired to build a Nim machine of my own. At this time there was little or no access to computing equipment outside the universities and research institutions. This was just after the age, as is often said, when there were only six computers in the world and nobody thought any more would be needed. So it was just a hobby.

I continued my classical studies and obtained entrance to Merton College at Oxford. Entrance to British universities, unlike American universities, was for a specific course in a specific subject. It was possible, but difficult, to change from one subject to another. In any case, I had studied mathematics only up to an elementary level, and had forgotten quite a bit of what I had learned. So I embarked on four years of classics. When I finished that it was 1958, and I was due to do National Service. Everybody knew that National Service was going to end the following year or maybe the year after.

My father, who had an unfounded belief in me, said 'If you can find yourself a place to study mathematics, I will pay for it'. Amazingly I did find a place to read mathematics, which I did for three years, but, I have to say, not very successfully. It was just too hard for me to catch up on what was effectively a gap of seven or eight years. Nevertheless, I spent three happy years doing that. Then when I finished, in 1961, I married and got my first job.

D: You mentioned your encounters with Strachey in 1950. Did you at that time see a machine, or was it just on paper?

J: For his pupils it was just on paper. There were some books about computing. One book, *Faster Than Thought* [4], published in 1953, contains a chapter by Christopher Strachey discussing computer programming of games. I had and still have a copy of that. So I read a few things about it. But I didn't have the good sense or the energy to think that I should make a serious effort to learn about programming.

D: Did you know Tony Hoare when you were a student at Oxford?

J: Yes, we were both at Merton. I went to Merton in 1954. We were both doing the four year course known as Greats: Latin and Greek literature, Greek and Roman history, Greek philosophy, and modern philosophy. Tony was two years ahead of me. We knew each other because we belonged to the same college, and there were many opportunities to meet. We both used the college library quite a lot, and often met there. Tony was very interested in logic. One of the final examination papers in philosophy was titled 'Logic'. This had very little to do with propositional logic, predicate logic, higher order logic, or anything like that. It focused much more on general philosophical questions. For example, a question about the raven paradox; or 'Is there a God?' One famous question was 'Question 7: Is Question 7 unfair?' That sort of thing. Tony was brilliant at this kind of thing; but he was also deeply interested in formal mathematical logic, and I learned a little of that kind of logic from him.

D: Were you very good friends?

J: I wouldn't say we were good friends at that time. Tony was two years my senior. In that milieu it would be slightly unusual to be close friends with somebody who was in an earlier year. Also, because he was two years ahead, we never went to the same lectures or tutorials. The classics course was divided into two parts. One was 'Classical Honour Moderations' or 'Mods', which took just under two years. The other was 'Greats', which took just over two years. So when I was doing Mods, he was already doing Greats. When I was doing Greats, he had already left Oxford and was studying Russian during his period of National Service.

2. Jackson Structured Programming

D: How did you get a job in 1961?

J: In one word: by nepotism. My father had a colleague, Maxwell Stamp, who ran an economic and industrial consultancy he had founded. He thought that computers would become important one day. Since I didn't know anything at all about computers, he thought I was just the person he needed. I spent a couple of months working on some economic statistics for a report the firm was writing. Then I was sent on a programming course for the Bull Gamma 300 computer. This was an electromechanical computer, programmed by wiring a plugboard. The course teacher was brilliant, and the machine was a lot of fun: it had a punch-card reader with five reading stations on the input track and could perform concurrent computations on the data in the cards as they moved along the track. One of the pupils on the course worked for an insurance company that had bought one of these machines. I suspect that they never got their system working properly: the machine was probably not reliable enough.

D: How did you use this training?

J: Eventually I did a couple of computing assignments for two of the consultancy's clients. These involved working full time at the clients' offices, developing the applications and their programs for systems that today look ludicrously small—but seemed quite challenging at the time. On the first assignment, for a bank, I did almost everything, even operating the machine for a couple of weeks before the newly hired operator arrived to run the machine in its newly built computing room. The bank had bought an IBM 1401 to replace their existing punch-card system, and the IBM salesman had done quite a bit of the application design, basing it on the old system. I was sent on a programming course for the 1401. That didn't take very long: the 1401 was beautifully simple. It was a character-based machine of variable word length, with decimal arithmetic and even mixed-radix arithmetic to handle the UK sterling currency. The store was only 4000 six-bit characters. It was very easy to program. Our machine had three rather slow magnetic tape drives, a card reader-punch and a printer. I completed the application system design, and wrote the programs. I took my programs, in the form of punch-card decks, to the IBM test centre in London and compiled and tested them there.

That all worked out very well. My programs seemed to work as I expected, with one salutary exception. One of the bank's customers decided to take away the job of managing their share register and run it on their own punch-card machinery. So we had to convert our tape file of their shareholder records to a gigantic punch-card file of 300,000 or 400,000 cards. This involved the slightly tricky problem of reformatting the shareholder names and addresses from the tape format of 30-character lines to the desired card format of 28-character lines. I was disappointed to find that in that huge collection of names and addresses there were some residual anomalous cases that my program design did not handle at all well. Still, my general—and, of course, very misleading—impression was that I could write quite reliable programs.

My second, rather larger, assignment was at the NAAFI (the Navy Army and Air Force Institutes), where the most important system was a very complicated payroll to be run on a Honeywell 400 computer. Now one might think that a payroll can't really be complicated, but this one was. NAAFI was an organization that provided canteens for all the armed forces. The complications arose chiefly from two obligations. First, whenever a hundred military people spent the night,

NAAFI was obliged to provide a canteen. So if a battalion went out on to Salisbury Plain for two days of night-time manoeuvres, NAAFI set up a temporary canteen for them. There were also permanent NAAFI canteens on Royal Navy ships. The second obligation was to comply with the Catering Wages Act, governing the calculation of overtime pay for people who work irregular hours in catering. The law was that each worker should agree with their manager their hours of work during the coming week, and then receive the overtime rate for all work outside those hours. So the punch-card payroll input for canteen staff recorded not only the hours worked by each employee but also the hours agreed with the manager day by day.

The Catering Wages Act produced endless anomalies because there were inevitably errors in the input data and comparison of agreed with actual hours—although simple in theory—became difficult in practice. The canteens on ships produced additional difficulties of their own. The ships were at sea, and there was no efficient data communication that could be used for payroll purposes. So the canteen staff were paid locally, on board. The local calculations inevitably contained many errors, and when the ship came back to port the weeks missed by absence had to be recalculated and the discrepancies resolved. Conceptually it was trivial but in practice it was rather difficult to determine and implement all the details.

D: So your first encounter with a computer was in 1961.

J: Yes. And it was wonderful. These machines seemed miraculous and completely fascinating.

van Vlijmen: Did you program everything in assembler?

J: Yes, both of those jobs in 1961 and 1963 were in assembler: SPS (Symbolic Programming System) for the 1401, and Easycoder for the Honeywell 400. There was a COBOL compiler for the IBM 1401 but our computer was a relatively slow and small model. The smallest 1401 had a store of only 1400 characters (hence the name '1401') and the largest had only 16000 characters. Even on the larger machines compiling a

COBOL program took an impossibly long time—so long that programmers testing COBOL programs usually fixed errors by patching the object program to avoid frequent recompilations. So I didn't use COBOL at that time.

D: You started programming in the 1960s. And at some point you also started writing research papers, right?

J: Yes, eventually: but that didn't happen until much later. I finished the second NAAFI payroll job in 1964. I left Maxwell Stamp and went to work for John Hoskyns, who was starting a consultancy in business and data processing computer systems. We did various jobs for customers, including some programming jobs. I had a little group of people and we began gradually to think about why programming was so difficult.

As I said earlier, my first job with the 1401 didn't teach me just how difficult programming can be. I did begin to learn that lesson with the NAAFI job: the informal ways of programming I used then were clearly not good enough. I spent a lot of time testing my programs, even working at night for a couple of months to get enough machine time. I saw that my programs had many errors, and that I could not honestly believe that I had found them all. So as the agreed date for starting operational running drew near I invented something I am proud of. The Honeywell 400 provided an operator's console in the form of a Teletype 33 keyboard and printer. When the computer was halted the operator could examine and modify words in store, and could even read and write on the tape drives. Program execution could then be restarted from any chosen instruction. So I added conditional halts to the program wherever I could see an opportunity to check for programming errors at run time. If the condition—effectively, an assertion on values of local variables—was not satisfied, the program would type a console message 'CHAOS at nnnn' and halt.

Because payroll output had to be sent promptly to the canteens, the NAAFI payroll was time-critical. The main payroll program took several hours to run, and there was not enough time to abort a failed run, correct an error, and rerun. So for the first few weeks, possibly more, of running the payroll I sat in a room next to the computer room from which I could see the operator. When the operator looked up at me I knew he had received a CHAOS message on the console. So I would take my program listings, go in, sit down, and try to see what was wrong in my program. I'd look at the local data, correct it, and make some program change that I hoped would solve the problem. And then we'd carry on. I don't remember the details, I don't remember how often it happened or whether it ever happened twice in the same run. But my recollection is that we never failed to get the payroll done, and that after a few weeks no more errors seemed to be occurring.

With this NAAFI experience behind me, what I knew about reliable programming was only that I didn't know how to do it. In my earlier years at Hoskyns it seemed that the key to a solution must be some kind of program modularity. Machines were increasing in size and larger programs were being written. Large monolithic programs—typically based on flowcharts—became very hard to develop and to understand, and modularity became a popular topic. A conference was held on Modular Programming in 1968—the same year as the NATO conference on Software Engineering. When we started thinking about how to make programming more reliable we had some very simple and commonplace thoughts. A program should be structured as a tree or possibly a hierarchy of routines that could be invoked; we specified a systematic way of defining the call interface. What did we do inside the routines? Well, we drew flowcharts originally and we had some kind of rules about the size and complexity of the flowchart. So this was a crude form of modular programming. Gradually we began to look more carefully at the large structures of the programs as well as the flow structures within routines.

One of the people working with me then was Barry Dwyer. He's now in Australia and he's a retired computer science academic. He was a control engineer by training, and he had a lot of good ideas. In those years Barry probably contributed more than I can remember. One remark I do remember quite well. We were looking at some typical data processing problem involving customers and orders. Barry pointed out that for one purpose the customers seemed to be higher in the tree than the orders, and for another purpose they seemed to be lower. I think this was perhaps the seed that later grew into the idea of basing program structure on input and output data structures.

D: Was this work in COBOL?

J: No, our work for Hoskyns was still mostly in assembler. Many people used assembler languages on the 1400, 1410, 1440, and on some larger machines, and many used the 360 assembler language on the 360.

D: Did you have any contact with the people who established and attended the NATO Software Engineering Conferences of 1968 and 1969?

J: No, not at all. The NATO conferences passed without our being aware of them at all. We just weren't part of that world. We simply didn't know what was going on.

D: Let me just quote you from your 1968 article [30] in Data-mation, 'The Meaning of Imprecision': 'Rigor and precision fail when the job to be programmed cannot be completely specified'. On the one hand, you were working in the field of data processing. From that perspective it makes a lot of sense that you noticed that formalizing a specification was often difficult, if not impossible. On the other hand, it seems that you were already comparing data processing to other application domains where formalization efforts had perhaps had some success.

J: I wasn't aware of anything outside my own experience, really nothing at all. In 1968 I didn't even know that there were academic people thinking about program design. I'd never heard of Niklaus Wirth or Edsger Dijkstra. Well, I knew about Tony Hoare because I had met him at Oxford. But it never occurred to me to find and read academic or research papers.

The basic idea in the paper 'The Meaning of Imprecision' was really not mine, it was Barry Dwyer's. You could say the problem was this: that in many data processing applications, particularly in things like payroll and sales, you have all kinds of anomalies. In payroll, the rules for paying employees would often be the result of an evolutionary process, a product of gradual and incremental interaction between government legislation, company policy, union agreements, and precedents and exceptions based on historical hard cases. None of these factors were formally specified.

Traditional manual systems dealt quite well with the anomalies by ad hoc decisions, but it was hard to reduce everything to formalized rules. You couldn't structure the rules in a nice hierarchical top-down fashion. Exceptions were a large part of the difficulty. In the 'Imprecision' paper, the point was that you could make decision tables, but you had to recognize that a lot of the structure was due to exceptions. The way to handle it was to check the exceptions first, before the general rule. This was a departure from a commonly accepted notion of decision tables, in which the action rows are ordered—the actions in the applicable rule are executed in sequence from the top to the bottom—but the rule columns are not ordered— the sets of cases they describe are disjoint, so the order of checking them does not matter. In this commonly accepted notion the table with ordered rules is formally inconsistent, because the rule cases are not disjoint.

Of course, the decision table semantics in which you check the exceptions before the general rules can be perfectly rigorous, precise, and formal. The only practical point is that the rules and exceptions seem rather chaotic in some ways, because they aim to capture the results of informal evolution. The relationship of informal reality to its description formalized for programming purposes is a large, very important, and much neglected matter.

D: The decision table in your 'Imprecision' paper can thus be viewed as a formal object, but its length is comparable to the length of the corresponding program code.

J: Yes, that's right. The decision table specification takes you close to a program that implements it.

D: Were names like ALGOL and Peter Landin familiar to you during the 1960s?

J: No, not at that time. I didn't begin to become familiar with any part of the academic computing world until the early 1970s. This happened gradually, partly as a result of the development and promotion of the program design method, and the giving of courses.

At the end of 1970 I left Hoskyns and started my own company alone. After a few months I was asked to give a program design course for a Hoskyns customer in New York City. In my absence during those months other people in Hoskyns— not the people in my old group—had put together material for a two-day course on program design; they sent it to me not very long before the course was scheduled. I looked at all the material and I thought 'Oh I can't teach this. I must create my own course material'. That was the beginning of turning my ideas into the program design method that eventually became Jackson Structured Programming (JSP).

I gave my course in New York to 20 or 30 of the customer's people. Their manager was very interested in technical concerns, and—I think—recommended me to the ACM office in New York as a potential giver of ACM Professional Development Seminars. I gave quite a few of these two-day seminars—perhaps about 20—in various cities in the USA, on trips of three or four weeks. At around the same time I was asked by a British company, Infotech, to participate in one of their commercial conferences on structured programming, where I encountered Tony Hoare again. In 1972 or 1973 that led to an invitation to participate in a meeting of the IFIP Working Group 2.3 on Programming Methodology, and gradually I met more people from the academic and research world. But that's another story.

D: Yes. I want to ask you about Working Group 2.3, but later. Tell me more about what you did in your new company, and about the development of Jackson structured programming. Were you still programming yourself? Did your programming experience continue to contribute to the development of your design method?

J: Yes, I was still programming. In late 1971 I recruited Brian Boulter to join my company. My original intention for the company had been to develop and sell software to support program design and testing. I had an idea for semi-automatic testing of COBOL programs by extracting test cases from the program text and instrumenting the program text to produce a trace of its execution against the test cases. Initially, at least, I did a lot of the programming for this product myself. Later, as the program design method became stronger and better defined, Brian and I together designed and built a preprocessor for making structured programs in COBOL.

We sold scarcely any copies of the automatic testing product, and the company's income depended almost entirely on our program design courses and seminars, which became quite well known. Infotech paid us to give a number of one-week program design courses, which brought us into contact with many customers and also with companies in countries outside the United Kingdom who sent people to our courses in London. Some of them wanted to teach our courses under licence in their own countries, and also wanted to sell the preprocessor to some of their own customers. The first licensee was Swedish, and eventually we acquired licensees in Norway, Germany, Holland, Italy and some other countries. The licensees' instructors were required to attend our one-week program design courses, and also to attend our instructors' course, which was originally for three weeks but later for two weeks only. It was the Swedish licensee who invented the name Jackson structured programming, usually abbreviated to JSP.

There was a very helpful synergy between our activities in developing the program design method, giving courses about it, and our software development. The courses compelled the development and incremental improvement of small examples and better clarifications of the design method, while—to use a Microsoft metaphor—the software development, especially of the JSP-COBOL preprocessor, made us eat our own dog food. The preprocessor was doubly helpful, because it was itself written in the language of its own source input, which embodied and even enforced the program design ideas. So we worked on the preprocessor's text in its own source language, pre-processed it into COBOL using the previous version of the preprocessor, and then compiled the resulting COBOL to give the next version.

D: Can you say something about this preprocessor? What were its chief features?

J: It provided a structured control flow language in place of the very awkward and error-prone COBOL control flow features. It separated out the executable statements from the control flow, and provided special executable statements for reading and writing sequential data streams. I don't want to turn our conversation into a lecture on program design, but I would like to explain the most unusual feature quite briefly.

D: Of course!

J: The feature is called 'program inversion', and is an integral part of the JSP design method. JSP design is based on describing the dynamic structures of input and output streams as labelled regular expressions. The sequential program structure is formed as a merge of all these expressions, preserving each one and merging them in the desired temporal relationships of reading and writing their elementary records. This structuring technique gives a very clear and reliable design for a sequential program. But conflict among stream expressions—a 'structure clash'—may prevent the combination of stream structures into a program structure. A familiar example is the impossibility of describing the calendar by a single regular expression in which both months and weeks appear as subexpressions. The clashing structures are then separated into two or more programs that communicate by writing and reading intermediate streams.

This kind of communication is familiar in the world of Unix and C, usually as a linear pipe-and-filter structure implementing the intermediate streams as Unix pipes at run time.

Program inversion is a compile-time transformation of a JSP program. The program is transformed into a procedure that upon invocation accepts the next record of a chosen input stream or produces the next record of a chosen output stream. The choice is made by the designer at compile time: if stream S is chosen the program is said to be 'inverted with respect to stream S'. The preprocessor input language provides standard open, close, read and write operations on streams. The COBOL language itself provides another part of the picture. The COBOL syntax 'select filename assign to TapeDrive1' binds the local name 'filename' to the physical device named 'TapeDrive1'. The JSP-COBOL language includes an elaborated syntax for the physical device name, allowing a chosen program inversion to be consistently specified in both the reader and the writer programs.

The design of a program P having n sequential streams is therefore, by varying only the file select sentences, also the design of the n possible inversions of P. An acyclic design separated into several such programs, P, Q, R,..., can be trivially combined into one tree structure whose edges are intermediate streams.

The notion of a stream is very general, as the wide applicability of process algebras shows. So program inversion can be seen as a general design technique. The task of designing a procedure to handle a stream on successive invocations for successive elements can be understood as designing a program to handle the complete stream and inverting it with respect to the stream.

D: Did giving your courses also contribute to the development of the design method?

J: Yes, definitely. Initially the program design method was novel, not at all well known, and definitely still a work in progress. So the reactions of the people attending a course might indicate defects either in the substance of the design method or in its presentation. These two aspects were intimately connected. Seeking a good way to explain the techniques and concepts of a method is itself a good way to discover its defects, and even to discover and clarify a better methodological structure.

D: Can you say more about this? How were the courses organized? What course material did you use?

J: The courses grew out of the two-day ACM seminars I gave in the United States. Those seminars combined lecturing, discussions arising from participants' comments, questions and—quite often—objections, and a few questions for the participants to think about. For program design examples, I presented each problem briefly and immediately proposed what I thought was an appropriate solution. Initially there were several topics, such as decision tables and large-scale design of a data processing system, in addition to the program design material, so there was plenty to keep me talking for two days. And two days was not too long to hold the attention of most of the participants.

The move to a five-day course was crucial. Usually there were between 20 and 30 participants, sitting in a room from nine in the morning to five or even six o'clock in the evening, with a lunch break and a couple of short coffee breaks. The way I found to hold their attention was really an elaboration of the methodological structure implicit in the design approach as it developed. Essentially the course consisted of a succession of small, but increasingly difficult, program design problems. For each problem the problem statement was explained, and the participants were asked to solve the problem.

The first problem was very simple: to design and write a program to print a multiplication table in upper-left triangular format. As the participants worked on their solutions I would walk round, looking at what they were doing and perhaps discussing it with them or offering a little help. Then I would present what I thought was a good solution, introducing the JSP graphical and textual notations for labelled regular expressions and relating them to a simple programming language. I showed the output structure and how it could directly form the program structure. After a little discussion I posed the second problem, which had two streams. This was a new difficulty. How could one program structure match two stream structures? The course continued in this vein, each problem introducing a new difficulty for which the solution I then presented introduced a new solution technique. I think it worked well because the course provided a succession of challenges combined— at least for the participants who worked hard—with a sense of progression, of getting something worthwhile out of the course.

More generally, I think difficulties are central to software development methodology. A good method must reveal the difficulties in a problem, help you to identify and analyse them and, if possible, offer a solution technique.

D: This was all on paper? There was no terminal in the room?

J: It was all on paper. The course material was on paper. In discussion and presentation I wrote everything on flip charts using marker pens. There was no projector, no ready-made slides, and certainly no computer terminal. Dijkstra proudly boasted in his preface to *A Discipline of Programming* [15]: 'None of the programs in this monograph, needless to say, has been tested on a machine'. Even if you don't sympathize completely with this boast you can surely see real value in insisting that confidence in a program design should rest chiefly on careful use of a sound design method rather than on testing.

D: Did you learn much from the reactions you received to your courses?

J: Yes, certainly. From one kind of negative reaction I learned that some people saw software development purely as a problem of mastering the technology environment. Some participants on courses—perhaps three or four out of many hundreds—were very proud of their very detailed knowledge of such intricacies of OS/360 as the control block formats and the mysteries of the Job Control Language, JCL. They made great play with this knowledge, and sometimes seemed to disdain a program design method as mere childishness. Of course, they rarely succeeded in learning the method and solving the problems simply because they wouldn't give it enough of their attention.

More helpful were the people who raised questions and objections that revealed ambiguities or inconsistencies or other errors in the course material or in what I was saying about particular issues or particular problems. This was tremendously valuable in improving the method and its documentation. I remember that one participant who had made many very good points during the course wrote in his course evaluation: 'I think I have been doing this kind of design for quite a long time: but this course has given me the concepts and the words to talk about it properly'.

D: Is it correct that your expertise was mostly in data processing, and that this was reflected in the course material?

J: Yes. My own expertise was almost entirely in data processing. But some of my company's customers worked in other areas, and we learned something from them by consultancy assignments, by having some of their people attending our courses, and in other ways. There were some applications of JSP to real-time embedded software, and to system software [52]. A software engineer in ICL, the computer company, used JSP for interrupt routines and wrote an interesting paper about it [49] in the company's technical journal. But the course material had a strong emphasis on data processing programs, partly because they allow example problems to be posed and solved with very few technical distractions.

D: Were the people who followed your courses of all ages? I assume they were all men?

J: I think most of them were probably in their 20s and 30s. Some perhaps were in their 40s. Nearly all the course participants were men. Most were either working programmers, or managers with strong intellectual interest who were considering adopting JSP in their development group. I remember one manager from Switzerland who was a good deal older than I was. I think he must have been in his sixties. That was exceptional.

V: How did people come across your work?

J: Our efforts at promotion were amateurish and never very effective. But there was a certain amount of word of mouth. Infotech, the company that promoted our courses as a part of their business, did quite a lot of publicity, and this led to some press publicity. The British government were looking to improve their programming work, and invited my company to teach some JSP courses at the Civil Service College. Later they adopted JSP, renamed, as their standard recommended method of program design.

Also, in the 1970s there was a widespread interest in structured programming. This was partly stimulated by IBM's promotion of their ideas about software development, arising out of a well-publicized project they carried out for the New York Times. Another source was an increasing awareness of the 1968 and 1969 NATO Software Engineering Conferences [7, 45]. Infotech ran conferences on software development for which they invited speakers from industry, from the administration, and from academic and other research groups, leading to a lot of interest in the academic work of Dijkstra, Hoare, and others, as well as the work of IBM people such as Harlan Mills and F. Terry Baker.

Some of this interest was technically superficial and ill-informed. More than once, in questions after a presentation at a conference some manager asked: 'IBM's method of struc-tured programming gives 62% improvement in productivity. What improvement in productivity does your method of structured programming give?' I was asked that question on more than one occasion. Of course I was tempted to say

93% or 87% or something like that. But I'm glad to recall my reply. I said that the improvement can't be measured like that: you must understand the methods being offered and choose the better one.

D: Did you and your colleagues use the words 'structured programming' in the late 1960s? I understand that the words 'Jackson structured programming' came from the Swedes later. But were the words 'structured programming' commonly used?

J: I didn't start my own company until the beginning of 1971, and don't think I had ever heard the phrase 'structured programming' at that point. Dijkstra's famous letter about GOTO statements [13] appeared in CACM in March 1968, and his 'Notes on Structured Programming' were first informally published in August 1969 as private communication EWD249. I didn't become aware of this work until later: perhaps when an enlarged version of EWD249 was published as the first of three parts in the 1972 A.P.I.C. book, co-authored by Dahl and Hoare [9]. None of my early two-day seminars for ACM or my early program design courses were described as courses in structured programming. Certainly the student handout for an ACM seminar I gave in 1972 is described on the cover page as 'Advanced Programming Techniques: Modular Programming Workshop'.

D: My impression is that you were not really influenced by the academics, like Hoare and Dijkstra. Did that only come later?

J: Yes. I'm not sure whether to be proud or ashamed that JSP was developed in almost total ignorance of the contemporary academic work on program design. In 1971, as I have said, I encountered Tony Hoare again, and he later invited me to write a book in the A.P.I.C. series of which he was the series editor. I delivered the book in 1974, and it was published as *Principles of Program Design* [31] in 1975. I was once accused of hubris in the choice of the book's title: but I was able to acquit myself by pointing out that the title was chosen by Tony Hoare.

D: I do notice that you have one thing in common with Hoare and Dijkstra. Just like them you say that optimization comes at the very end in software development. That's something you already said early on.

J: Yes. I proposed two rules for optimization. Rule 1: 'Don't do it', and Rule 2 (for experts only): 'Don't do it yet'.

D: In the 1970s, the words 'structured programming' had different meanings for various people. The commonality, however, was that optimization should come at a later stage in the software development process. Structure came first. You even wrote that, in general, you didn't optimize at all. Yet, most people in the 1950s to 1970s were trying to optimize their code, trying to fit it on their machine.

J: Yes. One dimension of optimization was space. Some of the very earliest machines had astoundingly small amounts of storage: for example, 128 24-bit words. I have already mentioned that the IBM 1401 was so named because its smallest model had a store of 1400 six-bit characters, which had to accommodate any necessary tape buffers, buffers of 80 characters each, for reading and punching cards, and one of 132 characters for the line printer, in addition to the index registers (which were in fixed locations of the store) and, of course, the machine code program and all its local variables. Even on the 1401 with a 4000 character store it could be hard to fit the program and all the data into that. In the latest stages of programming, you might be looking for somewhere to hold a five-character string, and so on.

The earliest machines with the very tiny stores usually had a magnetic drum on which the program was stored. This gave rise to a serious optimization task in the time dimension. To make the program run at an acceptable speed it was important to place the program's machine code instructions on the drum in carefully chosen locations to minimize—or, at least, reduce— the latency in fetching the next instruction from the drum.

I never did serious problems in numerical computation where time optimization was important. But I clearly remember one time optimization I designed on the 1401 that gave me a lot of pleasure. The application was printing dividend cheques for companies. Each dividend cheque had to be printed on one half of a page of which the other half carried the mandate to the shareholder's bank to credit the dividend to the appropriate account. For each company paying the dividend a magnetic master tape contained the shareholder records, ordered by the shareholder's number. Each shareholder had an account with one of five banks: Barclays, Lloyds, Midland, National Provincial, and Westminster. The printed cheques, with their so-called mandate information, had to be grouped according to the shareholder's bank so that they could be conveniently dispatched to the banks without manually sorting the tens of thousands of pieces of paper involved. The data for the cheques for the different banks were all interleaved on the tape.

An obvious way to do it was just to go through the master tape and print all the Barclays' cheques. Then rewind the tape and print all the Lloyds' bank cheques. Then rewind the tape again, and so on. But these tape drives were very slow to rewind: it took nearly 15 minutes to rewind a 2400-foot tape. So it would be a good idea to overlap the rewinding with the printing. I devised a scheme in which as the computer was printing the Barclays' cheques it was also copying the tape to a second tape on another drive. When a certain point was reached—I think it was about a quarter of the way along the primary tape—the copying ceased, and the second tape was rewound. At the end of the master tape, when all the Barclays' cheques had been printed, the second tape had already been completely rewound. Then printing of the Lloyds' cheques began, using the copied records on the second tape, and the master tape was set to rewind. When the master tape was completely rewound, it caught up with the second tape by reading four records for every record read from the second tape. Once the master tape had caught up, the printing could proceed again from the master while the second tape was rewound. And so on, iterating through the successive banks.

I was thrilled with this printing program. I remember standing in the computer room and watching the printer running without interruption except to replenish the paper. It was much better than having a toy train set. So that was my favourite time optimization, around 1962. Depending on the length of the master tape it could avoid a considerable waste of available computer time waiting for tapes to rewind.

D: So in the very beginning of your career, circumstances forced you to optimize.

J: Yes.

D: But ten years later, in your book, you wrote that optimization should be delayed, if applied at all.

J: Yes. How can I defend myself? First, of course, I did in fact delay the optimization. I started by writing the unoptimized version and only when I was confident of that did I create the faster version. Second, there was a clear separation of concerns available. The creation of each shareholder's printed output was completely separable from the handling of the records on tape. This kind of separation of concerns is a significant factor in restricting optimization to inner loops in certain kinds of program: an inner loop body may be consuming a very large proportion of the CPU time, and it may have a clear specification—a pre-condition and post-condition pair—that careful optimization can preserve. Both conditions, I claim, held for my tape rewinding optimization. So I plead not guilty.

3. Working Group 2.3

D: You became a member of the IFIP Working Group 2.3 in the early 1970s. Was that an important event for you?

J: Yes, it was very important. In the very early 1970s I was gradually becoming aware of the world of computing research, and of the possibility of more rigorous approaches to software development. I was invited to a few of Infotech's commercial 'State of the Art' conferences, where I renewed my acquaintance with Tony Hoare and also met some other academic and industrial researchers. I was invited to the 1973 meeting of the IFIP Working Group 2.3 in Blanchland, a village near Newcastle, and gave a talk there on my ideas about program design. At the end of the meeting I was invited to become a member of the group.

In that first meeting, and in later meetings, I soon came to recognize that the intellectual standards of the group were far higher than I had been accustomed to. Contributions to the discussion were more constructive, more knowledgeable, and more thoughtful than the hurly-burly of arguments between advocates of competing software design methods and tools in the commercial marketplace. If you gave a talk you were not considered to be delivering a lecture, but to be introducing a topic for discussion. Sometimes the title alone of a talk would provoke an hour of free-ranging, but very valuable, discussion. I enjoyed it all enormously. The contact with the academic world broadened my perspective.

D: In your writings you occasionally referred to the 1972 book by Dahl, Dijkstra, and Hoare [9]. What does such a reference mean? Were you merely acknowledging the existence of their work, or did their work influence your thinking?

J: Yes, of course the book *Structured Programming* must have influenced my thinking. I find it hard to know what has influenced me. Influence is rarely immediate, direct and obvious. Sometimes it comes from a phrase, spoken or read, that lodges in the subconscious mind and triggers a thought long after the phrase itself has been forgotten. Sometimes it comes from reading again a paper or a book that was read long ago but imperfectly understood. Dijkstra's writings, especially, repay repeated reading. Here's a tiny example. In the first part of the book he makes the point that to follow the progress of a computation we need some kind of co-ordinate system or index: the program variables, he says, cannot provide such an index because we can assign meaning to their values only in relation to the progress of the computation. This point is simple, obvious and brilliant. It explains concisely why a set of operations on a state is not, in general, a substitute for a structured program: if you haven't written the structured program explicitly you don't have a text pointer and you can't know whether the explicit state variables you have chosen are a sufficient substitute.

D: Did you already have these reflections on structured programming in the 1970s?

J: Perhaps not explicitly. But looking back I see that my work has chiefly aimed at achieving simplicity by structuring. Per Brinch Hansen called the 1996 collection [22] of his papers on parallel programming *The Search for Simplicity*. I like that. In JSP the idea of handling clashing data structures in separate processes is one example. Another is the allocation in a program structure of executable operations on data elements: if the program structure corresponds to the data structure there must be an obvious right place for each operation. JSP program texts also used the usual structured programming component types: sequence (or concatenation), selection (or if-else and case), and iteration (repetition and do-while). So in a sense we had at least some of these ideas already. But Dijkstra and Hoare articulated and illuminated them wonderfully well.

D: A precursor to Dijkstra's work on structured programming was his work on the THE multiprogramming system, which was quite differently structured. Tony Hoare co-organized a workshop on Operating Systems in Belfast in 1971 [25]. Randell and Brinch Hansen were present but Dijkstra was not. They were all talking about the THE system and its structuring in layers of abstraction. They were debating whether people should actually design big systems with such layers in mind. Did such debates occur in Working Group 2.3?

J: I don't recall any debates on that topic or, more generally, discussion of questions of large software structure. Perhaps my recollection is at fault. But I'm sure that interest in software structure was waning in the group in the first half of the 1970s, giving way to more formal, mathematical, concerns. In one way this seems surprising, because leading members of the group had done much excellent foundational work on software structure: layers of abstraction, object-oriented programming, structured programming, stepwise refinement, data abstraction—all of these have been tremendously successful.

But ironically the competing attraction of formal specification and proof may have played a large part here. A structured program in Dijkstra's sense organizes the text—and its execution—into a collection of nested regions, each having one entry and one exit point. This structuring greatly increases the value of program assertions: each region can be formally specified by a pre-condition and post-condition pair, and a proof of program correctness then has exactly the structure of the program itself. This possibility offers an attractive—even seductive—field of study and invention. Perhaps some of the most able members of the group were seduced.

One effect of the diminished academic interest in structure, and increased interest in formal specification and proof, was a widening split between academics and industrial practitioners. The academics were accused of failing to address the real problems of software development, the practitioners of failing to study and apply the academics' results. Some eminent computer scientists, I think, have now come to recognize that formal mathematical techniques don't address the largest and most important aspects of software development. As Tony Hoare said nearly 20 years ago: "It has turned out that the world just does not suffer significantly from the kind of problem that our research was originally intended to solve" [23, paraphrased].

D: Peter Naur is very sceptical about formalism in software development. Did you ever discuss the subject with him?

J: No, unfortunately I didn't. I think I attended only one meeting at which Naur was present; he dropped out of the group almost completely in the mid-1970s. But I greatly admire his work on the role of human intuition in software development and his scepticism about inflated claims for formal specification. His collection of papers in *Computing: A Human Activity* [44] is full of good things.

Mathematical formalism is essential for eliminating development errors of logic and calculation, and for solving certain kinds of optimization problem in design. But its primary use should be in a development context that has already been clearly structured by the use of intuition, experience and invention. In computing it is very easy to become seduced by technology—the most concrete and the most abstract. The concrete technology is the material technology of computing systems: CPUs, disks, screens, communication networks, and so on. The abstract technology is the technology of mathematical formalisms. Each can be far removed from the problem in hand. I remember at one meeting of the group an eminent member interrupted a speaker who was explaining a problem that he was going to talk about. He said: 'Don't go on talking informally like this. Just show us the formalism'. That must be wrong. You must understand and structure the problem first before formalizing it.

D: Many of your papers that I have here are from the 1980s. What Bas (van Vlijmen) and I notice is that you were repeatedly stressing a multitude of software engineering fields: compiler engineering, database engineering, and so on. Do you recall when you started to think like that?

J: Not, I think, before 1980. With hindsight, it should have been obvious to everybody. In establishing the 1968 NATO Conference on Software Engineering the Committee specifically identified 'the need for software manufacture to be based on the types of theoretical foundations and practical disciplines, that are traditional in the established branches of engineering'. But the conference report shows very clearly that the participants did not look outward to the established engineering branches as a model. They were scarcely mentioned, except by Doug McIlroy: his talk advocated development of a mass produced software component industry [45, p.138–155]. The most conspicuous characteristic of the established branches of engineering, and of their practical disciplines, is their multiplicity. But no-one mentioned it at the conference. I have discussed the multiplicity of software engineering with Dave Parnas for many years, but he is firmly resolute in his denial. In my opinion, the penalty for failing to understand the multiplicity of software engineering branches is failure to specialize. In engineering, specialization—of people, communities, education and methodologies—is vital to the kind of success we see in such everyday engineering products as cars and TVs.

D: Why did you start to think like that in 1980? Most other WG 2.3 members were advocating one methodology—at least that's the impression I have from reading Dijkstra's and Hoare's papers. So I see a mismatch between their work and yours in terms of ideology.

J: Surely people pick a topic of research that they think important; as they achieve some success they become more committed to their belief in its importance—and even in its universality. I think also that the distinction between problem and solution is a factor here. In software development the solution is always a computer program, so a general programming method seems to be the only necessary tool.

Of course, this is the syndrome of the small boy with his hammer. It's hard to admit that not every problem is a nail, and a hammer is not always useful.

The first hammer that came to hand for me was the JSP program design method. It does work really well on programs that produce sequential outputs from sequential inputs. There are many such programs, especially if the notion of sequential inputs and outputs is enlarged to embrace any time-ordered element streams—not just records on tape files, but also procedure calls, interrupts, communication packets, operator commands, events in some problem world, and so on. Program inversion allows the processing of such streams to be designed by JSP and implemented appropriately. You can try to push the boundary even further. Every useful program must have some input and some output, and a sequential program must traverse its inputs and outputs in some sequence. So you can start by inventing these traversals. But now perhaps the method is not really addressing the part of the problem that matters most. The game isn't worth the candle.

D: So was it the limitations of JSP that led you to see that different problems demand different methodologies?

J: I think the recognition dawned more forcefully when JSP was elaborated into JSD. JSD was a system development method for information systems of a kind common in the 1960s and 1970s. The core activities of these systems were manual: transactions and commitments taking place between people in the same or different organizations. All transactions were recorded, and the essential role of the computing part of the system was to support the correct and convenient recording of transactions and to provide information and other documentation about it all. A classic problem of this genre, posed as a challenge problem, concerned a lending library. The system must record acquisitions, disposals, loans, returns, fines for lost or overdue books, and so on. It provides management reports, reminders of overdue books, answers to such questions as who is borrowing this book, and other useful outputs.

The fundamental idea of JSD was to model the activity of entities in the real world by sequential processes in the computer. For example: processes modelling the life of a title, the life of a book and its loans, the life of a customer, and so on. The evolving states of these sequential processes model the state of the real world. On top of these model processes you add function processes, which produce regular reports and notifications, and answer questions. This is a useful separation of concerns. The world changes by manual activities; the model is updated to reflect the changes in the world; the information is derived from the model.

One little piece of the library system problem seemed awkward in principle: a requirement that nobody may have more than six books on loan at any time. This requirement doesn't fit into the JSD separation of concerns. JSD assumes that the real world activity is autonomous from the point of view of the computer, which is required only to record and model the activity. This new requirement demanded that the computer constrain the activity in the world, so it couldn't fit in.

Of course, the practical solution was not hard. When a loan is to be recorded, the computer simply produces a message forbidding a seventh loan, and the model process refuses to reflect a seventh loan. Focusing narrowly on the programming problem, there is no real difficulty. But that's a bit of a mess, isn't it? Now I would say that the problem didn't fit the JSD problem frame. In Polya's terminology [51] there was no principal part to which the new requirement could correspond or be assigned. At the time my discomfort merely planted the germ of an idea that grew into the later work on problem frames.

V: That discomfort was quite philosophical, isn't it? In your work you constantly ask the question what software engineering really entails. You were reflecting a lot from the beginning.

J: Yes, I suppose you could call my discomfort philosophical. Tony Hoare likes to cite Kurt Lewin's aphorism: there's nothing so practical as a good theory. I also like to think that in software development there's nothing so practical as a good philosophy—perhaps it's exactly the same point. It's worth saying that Kurt Lewin was a social psychologist: his theories didn't rest on formal theorems.

A proper theme in a philosophical approach to software engineering is to relate it to the established branches of engineering. Many years ago Tom Maibaum introduced me to Vincenti's book *What Engineers Know and How They Know It* [54]. It's a wonderful book. Vincenti worked as a practising aeronautical engineer for many years before moving to academia. The book is about the development of aeronautics from 1915 to 1945; it contains five extensive case studies—ranging from the most theoretical to the most practical concerns—and a treasury of careful thought about the nature of engineering. There are many lessons for software engineering. One case study is about what pilots of the time called 'flying qualities', explaining the problem of defining these desired qualities, and of designing airplanes that would possess those qualities. Solving these problems took about 30 years. Anyone who has ever thought about what are sometimes called 'non-functional requirements' of computer-based systems should read this case study.

D: Did you find that many members of the working group were sympathetic to your ideas? Didn't Brian Randell with his fault-tolerant work lean more towards your own views on software development? Randell, just to name one person, may have had some reservations about formalism as well.

J: I don't know if it would be right to say that Brian had reservations about formal work in general. His recovery blocks idea is brilliant. It cut across the layers of abstraction altogether because one way of looking at them—and I don't know whether Brian ever expressed it like this—is that initially every block is a recovery block, but with only one alternate and only an implicit acceptance test. If any block fails its acceptance test the whole program fails. This structure gives one layer of abstraction for the whole program. If nothing ever goes wrong it all works; but if anything goes wrong it all fails. Then you can start saying 'Well, actually, we could tolerate this bottom-level failure'. and you make one recovery block with a second alternate procedure to handle failure of the first. This first recovery gives a slightly fault-tolerant system. You could then make it fault tolerant all the way up to the top with restrictions depending on the application. So in a way you could look at this as a kind of refinement of the layers of abstraction, but you could also look at it as a denial of the layers of abstraction. I wrote a piece about this for Brian's Festschrift.

More generally, I think it's fair to say that few members of WG 2.3 now address large questions of problem and solution structure in their work. But they are an eclectic and open-minded group in general, and usually ready to listen to any idea that isn't absurd. So some of them are sympathetic to my work—at least to the extent of giving me a hearing. Cliff Jones has involved me in research projects aimed at bringing together formal methods to industrial practice. He and I and Ian Hayes have been discussing the problems of developing cyber-physical systems for many years, and we have co-authored two papers. I have always found Jay Misra very rewarding in conversation. Tony Hoare has always been supportive in many ways. I feel particularly grateful to Michel Sintzoff, who sadly died in 2010; he taught me much in several long email conversations. More recently I have had a lot of very enjoyable and instructive interaction with Manfred Broy.

4. Program Transformation Systems

D: How is your emphasis on problem and solution structure related to the general idea of program transformation? You have referred more than once in your writings to Burstall & Darlington's work on a program transformation system [6].

J: What I chiefly understood from Burstall & Darlington was the broad philosophy of that work. You should start with a transparently clear program in which clarity—and, of course, correctness—is the overriding concern. Then you transform it to reach a solution that has whatever other properties— for example, execution efficiency—you need. In this way you get a solution that may be very hard to relate to the problem, but if all your transformation steps were good, it must be a correct solution. That transformation culture allows you to say 'The structure of the problem does not have to be the same as the structure of the solution'. In a sense, that's all I have really understood of their work, but it seems to be fundamentally important. At one time the notion of 'seamless development' was fashionable in the object-oriented community. The ambitions of seamless development and program transformation are exact opposites. In seamless development you aspire to preserve a single structure for all development phases, using it to express everything from the problem statement to the statement of its solution.

D: Isn't what you are calling 'seamless development' a basic principle of structured programming? That is, to make solutions have the same clear structure as the problems they solve?

J: That's a very good question. Of course, the answer depends on what you understand structured programming to be. The emphasis in some naive presentations of structured programming is on simple top-down decomposition or stepwise refinement, in which the initial very abstract program is elaborated through several stages to give the finished solution text. At no point in this elaboration process is it envisaged that what was originally thought to be one structure—albeit in successively finer granularities—might turn out to be two irreconcilably conflicting structures. So if you start with a problem containing what in JSP would be recognized as a boundary clash you just grind on, level by level, squeezing one of the conflicting structures into the Procrustean bed dictated by the other. In the object-oriented world this is what the aspect-oriented people like to call 'the tyranny of the dominant decomposition'. They patch up the problem by chopping up one of the structures and distributing it in the form of band aids—therapeutically called 'advice'—to be plastered over the sore parts of the dominant structure.

Of course the more thoughtful advocates of structured programming did not fall into this kind of trap. Dijkstra's work contains two interesting examples of avoiding a potential conflict of this kind. The first example is from the THE operating system [14]. Full use was made of the notion of a sequential process characterized by its ordering of events and states, but not by its execution speed. Because the computer's peripheral devices operated at different speeds, and much more slowly than the internal computations, it was hugely advantageous to assign a process to each peripheral. The disastrously difficult—in fact, obviously impossible—task of explicitly interleaving all the processes in a single program structure was thus avoided. The second example is from Dijkstra's program to print, in ascending order, the first thousand prime numbers [9, Ch.1]. There he expatiates on the initial design decision to introduce an array of a thousand integers and to structure the program as a sequence: first fill the array with the primes, and then print the array. This was a very fortunate decision from the program structuring point of view: it avoided the difficulty of combining the conflicting structures of computing and printing the primes. When Knuth repeated Dijkstra's design for the same problem in his paper on Literate Programming [41] he adopted the same separation of clashing structures without discussion.

D: Are you saying that structured programming and program transformation are incompatible in some way? You have also referred in your papers to De Marneffe's ideas about program transformation, which Donald Knuth wrote about in his 1974 paper 'Structured Programming with go to Statements' [40]. The idea, in very general terms, was to have a structured program and gradually transform that into efficient and spaghetti-like code.

J: Certainly structured programming and program transformation are not incompatible: they share the ambition of allowing a program under construction to be understood as clearly as possible. Some early doubts expressed about structured programming—by Knuth, for example—questioned whether it might perhaps preclude the most efficient program designs.

De Marneffe's paper described a development technique based on 'holons', a concept drawn from biology. In programming, a holon is, roughly, a small self-contained unit of program functionality, including a test of its assumed execution environment in terms of data values. The primary advantage of holons as design components is their ease of understanding combined with an environment that ensures efficiency. The program is written as an assemblage of holons, and is then transformed into a machine-language program tailored for efficient execution by a particular computer. The transformation is somewhat similar to Knuth's later scheme of 'tangling' described in his 1984 paper on Literate Programming [41], but more powerful. But the literate programming paper was much later than his reference to De Marneffe's work in his 1974 paper [40].

In his mention of De Marneffe's paper, Knuth cited the engineering design principle, attributed by De Marneffe to Shanley, of collecting several functions into one part. He compared the WW2 V-2 rocket with the Saturn-B moon rocket. In the V-2 the outer skin, the structural elements, and the fuel tank are clearly distinct components; in the Saturn-B the outer skin serves all three functions. I think it's fair to say that neither Knuth's 1984 tangling transformation nor De Marneffe's assembly of a holon-based program satisfies the Shanley criterion. The essence of the principle seems to involve something more like a dissolution of the separate identities of components.

Burstall and Darlington's 1977 paper [6] gives a simple illustration of their ideas. Suppose you have a function that computes the scalar product S of two numerical vectors A and B of length n, so that $S = A \cdot B$. Now you want a function to compute the sum T of two such scalar products of vectors of length n, so that $T = A \cdot B + C \cdot D$. Their transformation scheme produces an interleaving of the two computations so that there is only one loop over the index values $0..n$. This, I think, is closer to Shanley's notion: the single traversal of the index values supports the functionality of calculating both scalar products, just as the single Saturn-B skin supports the functionality of multiple components in the more primitive V-2 design.

I have never heard Shanley's name mentioned except in De Marneffe's paper, but the principle is clearly at work in the history of automobile engineering. In very old cars you had a chassis frame supporting the engine, transmission, suspension and wheels, with a separate body mounted on the chassis to provide comfort, weather protection, a place for luggage and so on. The chassis and body were often built by different manufacturers. Now these components have been completely merged: the chassis is the body and the body is the chassis. In the same way, tyres used to consist of two parts: an outer cover, providing the interface with the road surface and some shock absorption, and an inner inflatable tube to keep the outer cover in its proper shape while maintaining its elasticity. The tubeless tyre combined the two, in one component providing the properties and functions of both; this is an almost perfect parallel to the rocket example. In software engineering we ought to pay more attention to this kind of thing; but we don't.

D: Is this combining of properties and functions the same as the design technique that the architect Christopher Alexander writes about? In writing about design [38] you used the word 'dense', quoting from Alexander's 1979 book *The Timeless Way of Building* [1]:

> It is possible to make buildings by stringing together patterns, in a rather loose way. A building made like this is an assembly of patterns. It is not dense. It is not profound. But it is also possible to put patterns together in such a way that many patterns overlap in the same physical space: the building is very dense; it has many meanings captured in a small space; and through this density it becomes profound.

J: Yes. I think this notion is important in many, perhaps all, design activities. A teapot, for example, must have many desirable properties. It must be easily filled; it must keep the tea hot, and hold it without leaking; it must stand stably on a flat horizontal surface; it must be easy to pick up by the handle and must pour without dripping; the handle must not become too hot to hold comfortably; the teapot must be easy to carry and easy to clean; it must have an attractive appearance. Each function considered in isolation is easily achieved. The virtue of a classic teapot design—that is, a normal design—is to combine all these functions in a way that reliably serves the needs of a significant class of teapot users. That's a central facet of its elegance and beauty: achieving much value with great economy.

D: Isn't this aspect of design, where you apply the Shanley principle to a car body or a teapot, different from the motivation to transform a clear program design into an efficient, but less clear, implementation?

J: Yes, there is a difference, but the Shanley principle is one kind of modification that in software, at least, can be achieved by incremental transformation. I imagine it's very hard to do this kind of transformation in designing a physical object because the material you're working with is not malleable in the kind of way that software and software designs are.

As I said earlier, I don't think we take enough advantage of this software malleability. There are many ways of looking at a complex software system, and many perspectives from which different aspects of its complexity can be understood. It's a mistake to suppose that just one perspective can be sufficient for all purposes. To choose a perspective is to abstract, and the essence of abstraction is to ignore—to throw away—what seems less important for the purpose immediately in hand. An obvious question about an abstraction is: 'What is the reality from which this abstraction was made? What has been ignored and thrown away?' An obvious danger is to give the reality only a perfunctory glance, and then rush straight off to make the abstraction. Premature abstraction is as harmful as premature coding.

So it's not just a matter of transforming a single program from one representation or structure to another, as in JSP program inversion. It's also essential to be able to handle multiple abstractions and to exploit their malleability to examine any relationship among them that is of interest. The JSP merging of stream structures is an example of this.

D: Apparently the enthusiasm for program transformation systems has diminished. Where did that idea go?

J: I think one part of it comes from an increased reliance on formal analysis. An assemblage of sequential processes is very difficult to analyse. There's a body of work on concurrency, interference, and so on, but formal proof of desired properties is apparently still very difficult. One response to the difficulty is to deny the importance of viewing such systems as composed of parallel sequential processes, and to see the system in a cruder abstraction simply as a set of operations on a state. This abstraction seems more amenable to formal analysis.

In some formal methods—like Event-B, Z, and VDM—the concept of a sequential process has essentially been discarded. This would be no loss if the development started with the sequential process view and then transforms the assemblage of processes to a state with operations. Of course, to preserve the behavioural constraints embodied within and among the processes, the state must include their text pointers and also a representation of the subset of processes running at any time; and the operations on the state must update the text pointers and the running subset. But there is often a serious loss if you construct the state without first clarifying the process view. For many purposes the process view captures essential human understanding of what happens in the system and how the system works. I remember discussing this with Ole-Johan Dahl many years ago. He said 'Sequential processes are completely fundamental because that's how we live our lives. We know that we have to get out of bed before we can brush our teeth, and we have to put our socks on before our shoes. Life is sequential processes'.

D: What's your view on Communicating Sequential Processes (CSP)?

J: CSP is all about concurrent sequential processes. Some people are working to combine CSP with other formal methods such as Z that abstract from the process view. CSP recognizes process structure, but abstracts from causality. In the world of a CSP system each process is ready to participate in some subset of the events in its alphabet, and—we may imagine—there is a deity constantly trying to do everything. An event can occur when those processes in whose alphabets it appears are ready to do it. So this totally abstracts from the notion of causality, from the idea that an event has an identifiable cause, with an active agent and other passive participants. So perhaps when two formalisms have been combined, both abstracting from causality, a third one will be needed, and then a fourth, and a fifth?

D: So, in the end, how important is the idea of transformation?

J: In the end, one way of thinking about it is in terms of a comparison with the established branches of engineering. It's true that their physical material is far less malleable than the intangible material of software systems, but perhaps they show us the way in another respect. They have many processes of many kinds, each designed for some specific purpose in some specific circumstances in the design, analysis, manufacture, assembly, and quality testing of specific products. If software—and here I mean the whole product of a system design—is more than just writing small programs, then surely we should recognize many opportunities in system development for a larger range of processes than we have now. Transformation is just a particular kind of useful process; there are many others.

5. Dijkstra's Pleasantness Problem

D: You are one of the people who are looking at requirements— the requirements engineering community. I'm inclined to summarize your work as bridging the gap between the informal and the formal world.

J: Yes, I agree with that summary. Have you read the 1985 paper 'The Limits of Correctness' [53] by Brian Cantwell Smith? He talks about the question 'Can you have correct cyber-physical systems?' (although he didn't use the term 'cyber-physical'). He draws a little picture. It's very simple: I can even sketch it here now (see Figure 5.1). There's the computer (C) on the left, on the right is the real material world (RW), and in the middle is a bridge between them: a formal model (M) of the real world. If you prefer, C is some algorithm or program, or even a reasoning human being.

Smith says that the relationship between C and M is the subject of model theory, but we have no theory of the relationship between the formal model M and the real world RW. He bemoans that lack and says 'It's hard to imagine what a theory would be and that's a major issue and it's not going

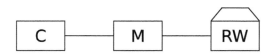

Figure 5.1: The computer (C), the formal model (M), and the real world (RW).

to go away'. The system cannot be 'correct' in any meaningful sense, because without such a theory the formal model can only be some kind of ill-defined approximation to the world.

D: In your 1988 paper 'Software Manufacture' you wrote that the bridge between the informal natural world and the formal system can be made only in an informal language. Furthermore, the bridge should be as narrow and as localized as possible, to ensure that the unavoidable informality does not spread to descriptions that have no need of it [32, p.4]. Is this another way of pleading for specialization in software development? What does 'narrow' mean in practice?

J: In talking of descriptive language, the bridge is what logicians call an interpretation: it's a dictionary that tells you what the formal terms in the model denote in the real world. It should be narrow in the sense that the denotations in the world, necessarily expressed in informal language, should be clear and exact; and the dictionary should be as small as possible, without synonyms or purely terminological definitions—for example 'sister = female and sibling'. This discipline can avoid a lot of confusions.

D: Would you consider having different models M of the real world RW in Figure 5.1? So far there seems to be only one bridge. But, in general, I guess you want to build multiple bridges.

J: Yes, you have put your finger on a crucial point there. In a realistically complex system there will be many functions and features and operation modes, and there is no good reason to suppose that the same model of the world will serve them all. In the early days of business systems, a company had a payroll system, a personnel system, and maybe it had a customer-sales system, an inventory system, and a supplier-purchasing system. These systems were often quite separate, even isolated. When a need for integration became clear, people thought this implied a unified model, an enterprise model. But of course that was very difficult—perhaps even impossible—because the different business functions look at the world in different ways that are hard to reconcile. So different models are needed, and reconciling and combining them is a major design task.

Exactly the same is true in a cyber-physical system. A very simple example arises from the need to tolerate faults in mechatronic equipment. You need at least two models. One models the mechatronic equipment when it is behaving faultlessly. The other models its faulty behaviour. The first supports the operation and use of the equipment for its designed purpose; the second supports the detection and diagnosis of faults. If fault mitigation requires a degraded mode of operating the equipment you may need a third model to support that behaviour. So, yes, you need many models.

D: You've probably come across this picture, Figure 5.2, in the booklet on Naur [10]. Dijkstra called this first step, from the informal design intent to the formal specification, the Pleasantness Problem. You have written about that topic (e.g., [37]). What is your reaction when you see this drawing? Is it a too narrow way of looking at software development?

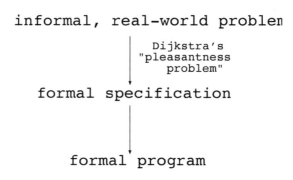

Figure 5.2: A copy of the figure on page 70 in the Naur booklet.

J: Yes, it's far too narrow for software development in general. But in this aspect of his work Dijkstra was contending against the view of the programmer as a craft worker struggling against unpredictable difficulties. He objected strongly to the word 'bug', which in computing had its origin in a real bug—a moth—that caused a malfunction in a relay computer;

rightly, he insisted on the word 'error', which clearly connotes a fault caused by the programmer, not by an intrusive moth. He wanted programs to be seen as mathematical objects, and programming as a mathematical activity, and advocated this view in brilliant developments of small programs solving such purely formal problems as GCD, Eight Queens, and listing the first 1000 prime numbers.

A notion of program correctness must assume a formal program specification. The question immediately arises: What is the significance of the specification, and where does it come from? Responding to comments on his paper 'On the Cruelty of Really Teaching Computer Science' [16] Dijkstra wrote that the formal specification is a firewall between the 'pleasantness' and the 'correctness' problems. The former—what program do we want—could be addressed by psychology and experiment, the latter—how to construct it—by formal symbol manipulation. This characterization of the problems and their treatment seems ill-considered: it relegates to 'pleasantness' the choice of Greatest Common Divisor in preference to Lowest Common Multiple, along with every other choice made in arriving at a formal program specification.

In a realistic system you can't separate the formal from the informal part perfectly. And in cyber-physical systems, for the reason Cantwell Smith gives, you can't achieve correctness of the whole system. But where formal correctness is locally appropriate for some purpose it doesn't make sense to allow informality to intrude on your formal demonstration that correctness has been achieved.

D: Peter Naur would also step away from the previous drawing (Figure 5.2). Instead, he would focus on this triangular relationship (Figure 5.3) between the real-world, the program, and the programming language constructs. In his drawing there is no distinction between the formal and the informal. And if the distinction must and can be made, then you and Naur both say that it is often wishful thinking to assume that

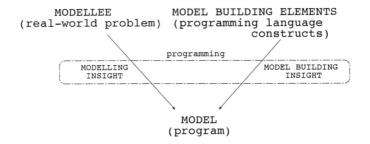

Figure 5.3: A copy of the figure on page 79 in the Naur booklet.

one universal formal specification language will suffice in practice.

J: Yes. A formal method of developing software has the same virtues and limitations as an arithmetic method of designing a house. You avoid logical or mathematical errors of some particular kinds, but you also close your eyes to a very large part of the problem you are trying to solve. By choosing a particular formalism you are implicitly abstracting away everything in your problem that cannot be expressed in the chosen formalism. Naur, I think, has made that point many times.

Perhaps I am more inclined than Naur to acknowledge the value of formalism locally and judiciously deployed. I think the crucial point is that in software engineering the role of mathematics is as the servant, rather than queen, of the sciences. You must first know what you want to prove or calculate before you set about formal proving and calculating. Didn't Gauss say 'I have my results, but I do not yet know how I am to arrive at them'?

The distinction between the formal and the informal is in any case very fluid in practice. Our natural language is peppered with elements of formalism; we don't hesitate in ordinary discourse to use natural numbers or refer to straight lines and circles or other figures of Euclidean geometry. And mathematical treatises, so far as I know, rely on a structure described in natural language to hold together their proofs and lemmas and other formal components of their argument and exposition.

D: On the one hand, we have the small mathematical problems, like the greatest common divisor, where a formal specification is feasible and short compared to the program code. On the other hand, this is not the case for the data processing systems where the formal specification is lengthy and rather chaotic. And for the cyber-physical systems it is not even clear if the requirements can be formalized at all.

J: Yes. For the greatest common divisor the formal program specification is feasible because the problem world—in this case, the world of natural numbers—is already perfectly formalized and all the properties relevant to the problem are perfectly well known. You don't start by saying to yourself 'What exactly is a number?' and 'What do I mean by one number dividing another?' and 'Can there be numbers that don't have divisors?' You learned all that in school.

But you don't have any such knowledge about the problem world of a data processing or a cyber-physical system. I agree that for systems of both kinds formal program specifications and system requirements are certainly lengthy, probably chaotic, and possibly completely infeasible. Actually there is an interesting distinction here between program specifications and system requirements. A program specification, as such, is about the computation to be carried out by a computer. The computer is itself a physical device, with internal capabilities for calculation, for storing and retrieving data, and for engaging in input and output at its external ports. All this is strictly bounded, and has been engineered so that the phenomena directly relevant to the program are unambiguous and reliable. A bit is 1 or 0; a line is high or low, and so on. Engineers have converted the continuous to the discrete. So in principle a formal specification of the program is imaginable, and so also is a demonstration that the program satisfies its specification. The difficulty is that for some programs the behaviour to be specified is too complex for human understanding; there are too many states and the transitions between states fall into no systematic pattern that can be mastered by abstraction or by a simple decomposition.

System requirements, by contrast, may be equally complex, but their domain is neither strictly bounded nor populated solely by reliable unambiguous phenomena. One stakeholder wants the system to appeal to prospective buyers in a market as yet unknown; another wants the system to be easy to operate; a third wants the system to be safe—avoiding all possible dangers to human life; a fourth wants reliable behaviour from physical problem world components whose behaviour can never be perfectly reliable.

You said, some time ago, that you thought I was a member of the requirements engineering community. Perhaps I should have qualified my response by saying that I am really a lapsed member. I don't believe that the classic notion of system requirements makes sense; that is, the notion that the requirements for a system can be captured and described in advance well enough to form the basis of an outsourced contract for development. This is possible for normal or standardized products, where the requirement can be described by giving a few parameter values that fix choices within the ranges of standard product variability. But for a largely radical product, development must be an iterative activity in which the developer and customer evaluate successive proposed versions of the product. In effect, the project is trying to enact a microcosm of what—in a certain sense—should be an evolution over many years or even decades.

6. Countering Top-Down Design

D: Can you explain why specialization is so important to you? Does specialization contrast to Dijkstra's generalization and the top-down development process?

J: It's interesting that you should make this contrast between specialization and top-down development. Specialization has many dimensions: specialization in problems, in products, in technologies, in methods, in applicable theory, and many others. Product specialization is vital because it leads to the evolution of normal design: design and development rest explicitly—and almost entirely—on what has been learned from experience. In car design, for example, the designer doesn't start from scratch, but makes an incremental improvement on a well-known established design. The opposite end of the spectrum is 'rethinking the motor car': relying on working everything out from general first principles.

Top-down development is paradoxical. It's advocated as a general technique in the form of top-down functional decomposition or—in the academic world—as stepwise refinement. But in fact it's not general at all: it depends on the developer's having deep specialized knowledge of the product class in question, even to the extent of being able to foresee the end result of the top-down process. If you don't have specialized knowledge of the end product you are aiming at, the top-down process is impossibly difficult. By definition top-down forces you to make the largest decision first. You have to design the top-level—at least in outline, at least far enough to identify the parts at the next level—at the moment when you know least about the design problem you are trying to solve.

D: Fred Brooks recommends top-down very strongly in *The Mythical Man-Month*. He writes there: 'I am persuaded that top-down design is the most important new programming formalization of the decade' [5, p.144]. You don't agree with him?

J: No, I don't. Although he writes enthusiastically about top-down he also recognizes its limitations from his experience with OS/360. He says that you often have to go back and scrap the top level because you have discovered something at a far lower level that contradicts your top-level design. This is also true of the stepwise refinement version of top-down development. In a refinement approach you have to begin with the largest abstraction. For a realistic cyber-physical system there may be no coherent large abstraction at the top level because the overall system function is an assemblage of many functions that must be individually understood before their relationships can be designed.

A beautiful example of this difficulty came up in a pilot design for a railway interlocking system. It seemed obvious to the designers that the top-level abstraction was a simple invariant: to avoid collisions there should never be two trains in the same track segment. They worked away for a time, developing several refinement steps, proving at each step that this top-level invariant property was correctly preserved. Then, quite late in the day, they realized that their top-level property could not be an invariant in any real system: it would make it impossible to assemble a train by concatenating rolling stock from two existing trains, and also impossible to rescue a train whose locomotive has broken down.

The physicist Richard Feynman pointed out the inadequacy of top-down development 30 years ago, in his work on the report on the Challenger space shuttle disaster [20]. His whole contribution to the report is worth reading, but he summed this point up in a final observation: 'A further disadvantage of the top-down method is that, if an understanding of a fault is obtained, a simple fix, such as a new shape for the turbine housing, may be impossible to implement without a redesign of the entire engine'.

D: Are you saying then that Dijkstra's examples of software development are poor models because they rely on generalized top-down thinking?

J: No, I'm certainly not saying that: I don't think they do rely on generalized thinking. The problem worlds for his programming examples are all well-known formal domains of mathematics, and of course he uses knowledge of those domains in designing his programs. For example, to print Fibonacci numbers in ascending sequence you know that computing $Fib[n]$ requires only $Fib[n-2]$ and $Fib[n-1]$. But to print prime numbers in ascending sequence you know that computing $Prime[n]$ requires at least all of $Prime[1]..Prime[m]$ where $Prime[m+1] > \sqrt{Prime[n]}$. I would say that these observations illustrate how specialization in a particular problem domain makes top-down development possible.

By contrast, in Dijkstra's account of the design of the THE operating system he makes a very interesting observation:

> Our first major mistake was that for too long a time we confined our attention to a 'perfect installation'; by the time we considered how to make the best of it, one of the peripherals broke down, we were faced with nasty problems. Taking care of the 'pathology' took more energy than we had expected, and some of our troubles were a direct consequence of our earlier ingenuity, i.e. the complexity of the situation into which the system could have maneuvered itself. Had we paid attention to the pathology at an earlier stage of the design, our management rules would certainly have been less refined. [14, p.342]

I interpret this experience as a close relative of the refinement problem I mentioned in the rail interlocking system.

D: In your 1975 book you wrote that 'components of general utility do not (and should not) emerge from top-down design' [31, p.36]. And in your 1983 book you emphasized that JSD is not a top-down method [28, p.370]. I'd like to delve more into your reasons for not working top-down. What can you do instead?

J: I wrote in the 1983 book that programmers who claim to be designing top-down are making a false claim: actually they create the program first in their heads and then write down what is visible to their minds eye. The essence of the matter is the ordering of decisions during development. With hindsight, this principle justifies the JSP design method: the input and output streams are known before the program itself, so it makes sense to start by investigating them and determining their structures before considering how their traversals may be combined in the program structure.

The alternative to top-down is, of course, bottom-up. In top-down design of a hierarchical structure the parents must be understood before their children: the identification and rough specification of the child is determined by its place in the parent. In bottom-up design the children must be understood first: the identification and rough specification of the parent emerges only when the children are understood. There is a beautiful illustration of this principle in Karl Benz's 1885 car, which is often considered to be the first true motor-car. Benz knew a lot about gas engines, and also a lot about bicycles, but a motor-car was a new, radical, design. You might expect that for stability its general form would be largely modelled on four-wheeled horse-drawn carriages, but in fact this 1885 motor-car had only three wheels. Benz was unable to design a suitable steering mechanism for a four-wheel vehicle: the unsolved low-level design problem of orienting the front wheels in a turn—what is now called Ackerman steering geometry—forced the top-level choice of a triangular plan for the whole car.

Another important principle of design processes applies to both top-down and bottom-up. Conceptually, the process should recognize two distinct phases in every parent-child relationship. In the first phase the structuring—whether top-down or bottom-up—should be loose, not tight. This means that the intrinsic properties of a component are determined before addressing the complexity of its interactions with other components. Feynman gives a good brief account of this approach in his contribution to the Challenger report [20].

D: In your 1983 book you wrote:

> Top-down is a reasonable way of describing things which are already fully understood. [It's] not a reasonable way of developing, designing, or discovering anything. [28, p.370]

This is very similar to what Peter Naur told me [10, p.45]. In mathematics, most mathematical papers are ordered in terms of lemmas and theorems, not in terms of how the proof of the main result was discovered by the mathematicians. If you were a mathematician, you would be asking your fellow mathematicians to publish in the way in which they had found their major results.

Niklaus Wirth even wrote in his 1974 paper 'On the Composition of Well-Structured Programs' [55] that he didn't really work top-down but that he was just presenting the solution in a top-down fashion.

Also Dave Parnas had a paper on this topic.

J: Yes: you must mean 'A Rational Design Process: How and Why to Fake it' [50]. That's a very good paper, it makes a very good point.

Really, the question is more general: 'How should a software design be described?' This must be answered with another question 'Why are you describing it?' Different answers to this second question imply different answers to the first question. You might want:

- to show an example of admirable design;

- to provide a tutorial example of applying a recommended development method;

- to provide a proof that the software satisfies its specification;

- to give a faithful historical record of the development process, including the reasons for adopting certain design choices that were made and also for rejecting others;

- to document the program structure, showing the interdependences among its parts, to make eventual modification easier and more dependable;

- to record the assumptions—particularly assumptions about the problem world and operating environment—whose future falsification may cause the software to fail.

Documentation separated from the compilable program text is hard to maintain without rigorous procedures for updating; so it seems attractive to keep everything in a single text. The challenge is then to structure this single text so that it can be read by many different people, serving many different purposes effectively. Knuth's work on Literate Programming [41] is a step in this direction. It's interesting that his TANGLE processor produces a Pascal program text that is not intended for human reading, but nonetheless the processor inserts cross references into the Pascal text that link it to the readable text from which it was generated.

7. Jackson System Development

D: Your 1983 book *System Development* is about Jackson System Development (JSD), which, as you wrote, 'may be seen as an enlargement of JSP, applying the same principles to a larger class of problems' [28, p.xii]. How were your programming principles enlarged to address the design of information systems?

J: In three ways, I think.

First, by enlarging the relevant context of a program to be designed from its input and output streams to the whole problem world in which those streams find their meaning. This enlarged problem world embraces not only the domains directly producing or consuming the streams, but also other domains of importance to the purpose of the system.

Second, by recognizing the importance of sequential processes more generally in the problem world of interest. As Dahl said, sequential processes are intrinsic to our experience of the world and to how we see it. I think I mentioned this conversation with him earlier in our discussion. Trying to build up a sequential process by fragments—by starting from the idea of operations on a state—is too difficult. Much of the relevant state may be hidden in people's intentions and transient purposes, in internal phenomena of physical domains, and elsewhere. This is closely related to Dijkstra's insight about program variables that I mentioned earlier: the visible variables don't provide adequate co-ordinates for understanding the progress of a computation because it is only by reference to the computation that we understand them.

Third, by seeing that the program inversion transformation can be applied to sequential processes in general. Specifically, to the processes that characterize the lifetimes of entities in the problem world—lifetimes that may extend over years or decades.

D: In the *System Development* book you not only covered data processing and information systems; you also mentioned embedded systems, switching systems, and control systems. But earlier in our conversation you said that your approach was really limited to information systems. Can you say more about that?

J: We didn't really recognize this limitation in the early stages of JSD. (By 'we' I mean me and John Cameron and other colleagues in my company, who developed the ideas.) The difficulty in the lending library system, of accommodating the requirement to restrict concurrent borrowing to six books per member, was apparent only to a methodological purist. It appears only when you insist on distinguishing indicative and optative uses of a problem world description. In an indicative use the description asserts how the problem world actually is, independently of the computing machine; in an optative use it expresses the desire that the problem world should be a certain way and that the machine should make it so. Development of a cyber-physical system, whose purpose is to impose some control on the problem world, demands both indicative and optative descriptions of the world. An information system, as JSD was originally conceived, merely observes the world, so its development needs only indicative uses of problem world descriptions. The optative descriptions describe the production outputs of the system, not the problem world.

D: In the book you wrote that a system is a simulation of the real world. [28, Ch.1].

Was this not a fairly obvious view? Yet my impression is that this is not something one would find in many other books of the early 1980s. Why were you emphasizing this?

J: I think because I wanted to emphasize the importance of being very clear about the subject matter and purpose of each development step and each development description. In structured analysis, context diagrams showed the system—that is, the machine—plus the 'terminals', which are the parts of the problem world communicating directly with the system. But there was no description or analysis of what went on in the terminals or of communication among them or with other parts of the world. This focus on the machine was very deeply embedded in most thought about computing systems, and very persistent. In a keynote talk at ICSE in 1995 [35] I discussed the relationship between the problem world and the computing machine. I pointed out that descriptions of the machine were often given under the pretence of describing the problem world—a kind of wolf in sheep's clothing. This is especially true of object-oriented methods.

D: One reason for viewing the system as a simulation of the real world was your emphasis on creating the model of reality before creating the system functions, wasn't it? You claimed that the model is more stable than function. You wrote: 'If the view of reality changes, the functions must change, but not vice versa' [28, p.12]. How did you justify this?

J: Of course model and function are interdependent: the model supports the function, and the function necessitates the model. The primacy of model over function is a matter of breaking this circle at its most readily breakable point. Also, model really is more stable in very many systems, where the function may be largely within the discretion of the owner of the system, while the model may involve the larger world and is therefore more resistant to change. Another consideration is that usually one model serves many functions. So by starting with one function you risk creating an arbitrarily limited model that is very hard to escape from later.

D: In the 1983 book you stressed that a software developer should start by creating the specification as opposed to starting from a specification. Presumably this was an unorthodox division of responsibilities. Didn't developers expect to receive a specification from system analysts, or even from customers, not to develop one for themselves?

J: Yes, they usually did. But the kind of specification that was common among software developers focused on the solution implementation rather than on the problem. In a typical system the gap between the problem and the solution was large, and could be bridged only in many development steps. Communication between problem owners and solution developers was hampered by the lack of a commonly understood way of bridging this gap, or even of identifying the ends of the gap. Software developers often felt that the problem, as seen by its owners, was not their responsibility and therefore not really their concern. Barry Boehm characterized this established attitude of software developers like this. He described the software engineers 'sitting on the side, waiting for someone else to give them a specification they could turn into code' [3].

My feeling was, first, that the gap could be understood—at least, in principle; second, that this understanding rested largely on concepts of software transformation and was therefore chiefly the responsibility of the software developers; and third, that an understanding in principle would be enormously helpful in practice, avoiding many confusions and difficulties.

D: I understand that program inversion was a very important technique. But how does that relate to your emphasis on the real world and the problem?

J: Program inversion forms the essential link between the behaviours in the real world—the 'long-running programs' that represent entity life histories—and arbitrary scheduling of recording and responding to events in those behaviours by such software functions as file updating. If you ignore the real world, file updating looks trivial. In chapter 15 of *A Discipline of Programming* [15] Dijkstra castigates business programmers for thinking that file updating is hard. He shows a solution, demonstrating that it is really very easy to coordinate the reading and writing of the sequential files involved. But this solution completely misses the real point of the problem. The difficulty is not in the file manipulation but in the logic of updating a master file record from the transactions that have occurred since the previous updating.

You can think of the problem like this. The life history of a customer, or a product, or a supplier, or an order, or whatever the master file record is about, is a sequential process executed over many days, weeks, years or decades. The input stream to this process is the complete stream of transactions over the whole lifetime. In the weekly file updating program you are required to apply an arbitrary subsequence of this input stream—a segment comprising exactly the transactions since last week—to the state of the master record resulting from last week's updating. The problem is to perform this updating correctly. The JSD solution is to regard the whole life history as one sequential program to which the transactions form the input stream. Invert this program with respect to its input transaction file, and recognize that the master file record is the saved state of the inverted program. Without program inversion or an equivalent—perhaps, one based on continuations—this is a seriously hard problem. To see how hard it is, think of the formal grammar of a simple programming language. Given this knowledge, then write down the grammar that defines every possible twenty-five-character substring of a program in the language. That is the file updating problem.

D: In your writings, you repeatedly stressed that most software development techniques, like UML, model in terms of the solution. From your first book onwards, you emphasized that a software designer should look at the real world. If I understand correctly, it was kind of natural to do that in the JSP data processing context. And then you continued doing that in subsequent years.

J: Yes. And in my work on Problem Frames I am still working on that very general principle.

D: In your 1983 book, you also stressed the difference between automating and deferring making decisions [28, p.26]. Often they go together. For example, a compiler optimization is both automated and happens after the programmer has made his programming choices. You've stressed in your writings that they don't have to coincide and that deferring decisions is more important than automating them.

J: Yes. One of the most important lessons for software developers is patience: doing things in the right order. This means, above all, recognizing the steps in the exploratory and intellectual journey that a software development involves, and giving each step its due weight.

Some software developers like to do certain things prematurely. They want to rush ahead to the task they like best, and when that is done they don't want to do anything more. Because they see themselves as developers of software above all, the most common favourite task is program coding and debugging. This is the underlying motivation of the more extreme practitioners of the agile movement. They disdain requirements, which they would like to reduce to so-called 'user stories'—a few words scribbled on cards. They don't approve of specifications, preferring a small set of test cases. And they certainly don't like to provide documentation of their programs. The only thing that matters is the program code.

Some practitioners of formal methods behave similarly. Effective use of formalism in software engineering presupposes a lot of informal preliminary work to identify, explore and structure the problem. Formalism can then bring rigour and mathematical verification to those parts of the informal work that may contain errors of logic or calculation. Extreme proponents of formal methods are inclined to skimp on the informal preliminary work because they consider it of little or no interest: they want to rush to their preferred activities of formal manipulation and proof.

D: You wrote that, by deferring, the concerns are removed from the specification to the implementation, so from the 'what' to the 'how' [28, p.25–26]. But, at the same time, 'the specification should in principle be directly executable' [28, p.28].

J: Yes, this may seem paradoxical. Perhaps the phrase 'directly executable' is misleading. Or perhaps the word 'specification'. I think the sense in the paradox is that if a specification describes a sequential process, or more generally, a behaviour, it should do so in terms that preserve its human comprehensibility. In particular this holds for the ability to execute entity behaviour descriptions even if execution of the real behaviour takes years or decades.

D: You've stressed that 'the specification is written in user's terms' [28, p.28]. So the specification is expressed in terms of the real world and it is executable at the same time.

J: Yes. The events in the executable behaviour specification are clearly real problem-world events and clearly recognisable to the people familiar with that world.

D: In your 1983 book, you also distanced yourself from both testing and proving correctness. Specifically, you wrote that proving correctness does work if the specification can be carried along with the proof and that only works if the specification is very short—which is typically not the case in the data-processing area [28, p.27]. Furthermore, your 1975 and 1983 books are not about testing.

J: In his preface to *A Discipline of Programming* [15] Dijkstra proudly asserted that none of the programs in the book had been tested on a computer: confidence in the correctness of a program should be established by other means. Two questions arise here: What is 'correctness' for a program? What can establish the desired level of confidence? If correctness is formal satisfaction of a formal specification then testing is certainly inadequate, and arguably unnecessary or even undesirable. If correctness is evoking a satisfactory behaviour in the material problem world, resulting from interaction with the computer, then testing is absolutely essential: the material world, at the granularities of interest in software engineering, is not a formal system. To turn Dijkstra's famous observation on its head, we should say that in a cyber-physical system, where the computer's purpose is to exercise control over the material world, formal reasoning can demonstrate the presence of error, but never its absence.

I think also that formal reasoning in programming should go hand-in-hand with intuition. Following Hoare's brilliant aphorism, our software should be so simple that it has obviously no errors, rather than so complex that it has no obvious errors. Simplicity was certainly the core of the JSP program design method: by structuring the program to reflect the data streams, JSP ensures a natural place for every operation on those streams and on each of their components.

D: You wrote that 'process scheduling [is] determined when the system is built, rather than when it is run' [28, p.37]. This is related to the program inversion technique that we've already discussed. So this is fixed scheduling.

J: Yes. When a JSP program is decomposed into two or more processes to resolve a structure clash, the processes could be regarded as concurrent processes to be synchronized. The largest possible granularity of synchronization is the complete intermediate stream: first the whole stream is written, then it is read. But a much finer synchronization is usually desirable: the obvious finer synchronization points are the read and write operations on the intermediate streams. Program inversion makes this fine synchronization practicable and allows it to be bound at design time.

D: Fixed scheduling makes things easier. Moreover, there is no need for recursion in these data processing applications. Based on Hoare's formalization of your JSP method [24], regular expressions suffice to capture your methodology.

J: Recursion does play a role in specification for some data processing applications. For example, in a genealogy application the concept of an ancestor is important: an ancestor of a person p is a parent of p or a parent of an ancestor of p. It also has a role in programs involving tree exploration more generally. For example, backtracking problems that involve exploration of a tree whose leaves are candidate solutions.

In the JSP method regular expressions are, above all, a tool for understanding structure. They are a very good tool for this purpose because they allow processes, and behaviours more generally, to be understood in nested regions. You can look at a part of a structured program and ask: What is this part's function? In what context is this function performed? The structure makes it easy to ask and answer these questions. In a flowchart it's much harder. It's hard to isolate regions for consideration, and even harder to see the context of any part of a flowchart.

For this structural use, regular expressions are not formally sufficient. For example, a stream structure may contain an iteration of parts, each part associated with one customer, the records belonging to one part being enclosed between header and trailer records of particular kinds. That can be perfectly described in a regular expression. But in another case, the records of each customer part may be distinguished only by carrying the same unique customer identifier. That's not formally a regular expression. But in practice the structure is easy to parse, so the structural advantage is not impaired.

Unfortunately these simple ideas are not common currency in program development. My son Daniel told me of a lecture by an eminent computer scientist. The lecturer presented a small problem, saying 'Here's a problem that's caused me a lot of trouble', and showed his solution. It was a simple JSP problem, and his solution was ridiculously confused. I find that very disappointing.

D: In your 1983 book you wrote that you don't talk about data processing any more but about events in general. So, the data structures in the real world also help you design embedded systems?

J: Yes. The fundamental notion of a sequential stream of elements transfers exactly into an embedded system where you have sequential streams of events. There is the considerable added complication that the physical components in the problem world can't be pulled apart so easily as record streams in a JSP program. So it is necessary to consider behaviours, where a behaviour is an assemblage of sequential streams of events in interaction components. Decomposition into regular expressions is still a very valuable tool: the regular expressions have many uses as projections of the overall system behaviour.

D: In your 1988 paper 'Software Manufacture' you explained that there are complementary ways of looking at our field:

1. a program can be viewed as a mathematical object,
2. software can be seen as an engineering product,
3. software development can be perceived as
   (a) a special case of knowledge engineering,
   (b) a human social activity, or
   (c) a manufacturing activity.

Like Peter Naur, you then explained these viewpoints in terms of 'descriptions' [32]. What, then, do you mean by 'descriptions'?

J: I like the word 'description' because it emphasizes the fact that software engineering faces in two directions. Everything we do is expressed by writing a description in some graphic or textual notation. And each of these descriptions has a meaning in some part of the universe we are concerned with in building a system. All these descriptions must eventually be manipulated and compared, reconciled, or combined in some way, both to produce executable software and to demonstrate convincingly that executing it on computing machinery will have the effect we want in the world. But this is a very general view, and the devil, as always, is in the detail.

One of the difficulties in thinking about software is its huge variety. A function definition in a spreadsheet cell is software.

A smartphone app is software. The flight management system for an Airbus A380 is software. A word processor is software. A communication protocol is software. We shouldn't expect a single discipline of software engineering to cover all of these, any more than we expect a single discipline of manufacturing to cover everything from the Airbus A380 to the production of chocolate bars, or a single discipline of social organization to cover everything from the United Nations to a kindergarten. Improvement in software engineering must come bottom-up, from intense specialized attention to particular products. Vincenti has a wonderful case study about the problem of flush riveting for aircraft skins. It took 20 years and the cooperation of several aircraft companies to find a satisfactory solution.

8. AT&T

D: Let's discuss your cooperation with Pamela Zave at AT&T. How did it come about?

J: Dave Bergland, the manager of Pamela's department, was very interested in software design methods. In 1981 he published an article [2] in which he argued strongly for JSP. He had attended one of our courses, taught by John Cameron (who was working with me in my company on the development of JSD). At some time in the mid-1980s he offered John the opportunity of a six-month visit to Bell Labs in New Jersey to work on the call processing problems of telephony. John accepted, and spent six months working on applying our ideas to those problems. He gave a little example of his work in his tutorial volume [8] on our methods. A year or so after John's return I met Dave at a conference. He asked what I was doing, and I told him that I was about to leave my company and work independently. He then offered me a consultancy contract to work in his department with Pamela for six one-week visits per year. I accepted eagerly, and our cooperation continued on that basis for about 12 years.

D: Was the problem clearly defined from the outset?

J: In one sense it was, and in another sense it wasn't. The problem had emerged from the success of electronic telephone switches, which replaced the earlier relay systems. The electronic systems were effectively general-purpose computers programmed in C, controlling the switching of voice and control circuits at an exchange. Competition among companies building these switches led to proliferation of calling features—call forwarding, call blocking, voicemail, automatic callback, call waiting, conference calling, and very many others. Telephone company customers subscribed to many features, and expected them to be easily combined in whatever way seemed useful. The emerging problem, quickly recognized throughout the industry, was the feature interaction problem. Features interacted in unexpected ways, often puzzling and exasperating the telephone subscribers. This was clearly the problem. It was very important because the software in the switches had become unmanageably complex, and threatened to make further development intolerably expensive and eventually, perhaps, impossible. What to do about it was not clear.

D: How did you and Pamela address the problem? Where did you start?

J: We started by talking about calling features. I knew little or nothing about them, and Pamela described and explained many features to me. We described them in various notations and formalisms: in JSP structure diagrams, in a modified version of them devised by Pamela, in Statecharts, and in different flavours of flat and structured state machines. We also talked more generally about software systems and the relationship of the software to the problem world. To these conversations I contributed some of the ideas I was working on at the time, which eventually appeared in my book *Software Requirements & Specifications* [34], so our discussions and work ranged quite widely. We published a paper on the structure and composition of specifications [58], and we were both active, along with other people, in promulgating the idea of requirements engineering, starting the first conferences on the topic and contributing papers, and in founding the IFIP Working Group—WG2.9—on Requirements Engineering. Pamela surveyed the nascent field in her paper 'Classification of research efforts in requirements engineering' [56].

We continued to work on this topic, and it progressed more or less in parallel with our work on the feature interaction problem.

D: How valuable was this work on requirements for the work on telephone features? Was there a very close connection?

J: No, I don't think so. Really, we were rather stuck on the feature interaction problem, like everyone else whose work we knew of. But in 1996 we had an inspiration. We were talking about the 1-800 numbers. If you call, for example, 1-800-AIRWAYS your call goes through to British Airways, and the callee pays for the call, not the caller as is normally the rule. Pamela explained to me how this works. The call goes to a special '800-server' node in the network that resolves the destination address to the real British Airways number and passes on the call, like a domain name server, but in a circuit-switched world. The inspiration was simply to ask why this should not be the basic pattern of calling features in general: each feature—like 1-800 calling—would have its own server nodes. Of course, these server nodes would be virtual, not physical, but the principle would be the same. Virtual nodes would be created dynamically, and connected by virtual calls over virtual voice and control circuits established by a software router.

This turned out to be a really good idea. The node classes correspond to features. Conceptually the features are orthogonal. Feature instances are assembled dynamically into *usages* according to participants' subscriptions and run-time conditions and commands. Precedence among features can be controlled by their order of assembly, which might vary between subscribers. Imagine, for example, a callee who subscribes to call-forwarding and to voicemail. If the callee is busy when a call arrives, the callee's line interface returns a busy signal. If the call-forwarding node is closer to the line interface it receives the busy signal first, and the call will be forwarded, otherwise it will go to voicemail. If the call-forwarding feature is closer, but has been de-activated by the subscriber, it will pass the busy signal back to the voicemail node and the call will go to voicemail. Mutatis mutandis, the same is true for the reverse node order.

We called this Distributed Feature Composition, or DFC, and published a paper about it [29] in 1998. We wrote multiple papers about various aspects and extensions and implications of the scheme. We received several patents. Pamela made some brilliant extensions, especially in the area of mappings between subscribers and addresses. She also worked on formal proofs of some of our feature specifications, using Spin [26] and Alloy [27]. We designed a programming language for feature nodes. Altogether we had a lot of fun.

D: How do these telecommunication applications differ from the other three, which we have already discussed:

- the 'small' mathematical problems,
- the data processing systems, and
- the cyber-physical systems?

Did you have the impression that Zave's case studies were immensely difficult, or did you quickly recognize various kinds of structure that you were able to exploit?

J: The difficulty in the problem that Pamela and I were trying to address—the interaction problem for calling features in a telecommunications system—lay entirely in the interactions: the individual features were not complex. The complexity due to the feature interactions was a huge practical problem in at least two ways.

First, it made a large contribution to program crashes, which threatened the required availability of the whole switch. This aspect was solved early on by exploiting the special nature of the telephone system. Telephone calls have a special episodic nature: their granularity has something in common with the idea of a transaction in a database system. This allowed the software architects to save themselves from the consequences of complexity unmastered by the program designers. The switch ran a perpetual audit process that checked the local data structure associated with each call against certain specified invariant properties. Any call not satisfying its invariants was potentially liable to cause a program crash, and was simply disconnected. Because calls are largely mutually independent the effect of the disconnection was narrowly contained. The disconnected caller and callee would be unaware of the narrowly avoided failure: they would attribute it to finger trouble or to some fault in the line, and simply try again.

The second effect of the feature interaction problem was more serious. It threatened AT&T's continuing ability to dominate the market for telephone switches by offering exciting new call-processing features. The software was becoming unmanageably complex, and there was a danger that it would become completely impossible to add new features. The root of this difficulty was partly conceptual, located in the basic notion of a call. In the earliest telephone systems the idea of a single telephone call was easy to understand. The caller calls. If the callee answers they talk, and when they have finished talking they hang up and the call ends. If the callee does not answer the call ends without their talking. When computer-based switches allowed a multitude of interaction features, the idea of a call, with one caller and one callee, became untenable. Pamela published a paper on this subject, entitled 'Calls Considered Harmful' [57].

One attempt—not ours—to find a better structure was based on the idea of a 'half-call', intended to capture the participation of one subscriber rather than of two. But it turned out that half-calls were not much more tenable than calls. The DFC work restored the original simple idea of a call, but only as a virtual link between features or between a feature and a line interface; the dynamic structure formed by these links was not a 'call' but a 'usage'. Viewed statically, the structure of a usage had something in common with the structure of a system based on a pipe-and-filter architecture, like a large JSP program. But of course a vital point was that it was completely dynamic.

D: You said that in parallel with the feature interaction work you continued your work on requirements and specifications.

Did that work have an impact among your colleagues in Bell Laboratories?

J: Very little, in spite of Pamela's efforts to interest people in it. However, we did spark some interest in Carl and Elsa Gunter, two AT&T researchers. We talked to them quite a lot about requirements. In my book *Software Requirements & Specifications* [34] I had explained the idea that a system comprises a machine and a problem world: the system requirements R are about the problem world, which has its own given properties D. For a successful specification S of the machine's behaviour in its interactions with the problem world, the entailment $D, S \vdash R$ must hold. That is: installing the machine in the world must cause the world to satisfy the system requirements.

Carl and Elsa liked this idea and naturally, being formalists, they wanted to formalize it. Eventually a joint paper [21] was published in 2000 by Carl, Elsa, Pamela, and me, giving a formal model of the relationships between machine and problem world, and between requirements and specifications.

9. Problem Frames

D: The entailment $D, S \vdash R$ is the foundation of your work on problem frames, isn't it? Did that emerge from your work with Pamela Zave?

J: Yes, the basic distinction of the machine from the problem world and the problem world requirements from the machine specification, and the reasoning necessary to develop the specification from the requirements, were all there in our 1995 ICSE paper 'Deriving Specifications from Requirements: an Example' [39] and the 1997 'Four Dark Corners' paper [59].

The significance of the entailment is that in a system of the kind we were discussing the problem world has given properties D, and the machine has properties S due to its software. When you put them together, you get some behaviour that is what you require (the requirements R).

D: Apparently the take-away message of Anthony Hall in the book *Software Requirements and Design: The Work of Michael Jackson* [48, Ch.8] is that the entailment $D, S \vdash R$ implies that requirements can be formalized. So the real world can be formalized! This is expressed in this diagram you use in your paper 'The Name and Nature of Software Engineering' [37], isn't it?

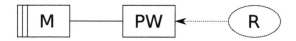

Figure 9.1: A graphical representation of the entailment $M, PW \vdash R$, alternatively denoted as: $D, S \vdash R$.

J: Yes. Before I answer your question, let me just clarify a trivial point of notation. The entailment has been mentioned and discussed in several contexts and several papers and talks, with many variations in the words used to denote the machine and the problem world. Sometimes the machine is M, sometimes it is the specification S. Sometimes the problem world is the application domain D, sometimes it is the world W, sometimes it is our knowledge K of the world's given properties. Each time the choice of the letters in the entailment is influenced. So for the graphical representation in Figure 9.1 the entailment might be written '$M, PW \vdash R'$. It's unforgivably confusing.

Turning to your question about formalization, there is an important distinction between formalizing the requirements and formalizing the real world—or, at least, the parts of the real world that are included in the problem world. For me, this has emerged clearly only in the past few years. The diagram of Figure 9.1, and the entailment, clearly indicate that the effect of the machine, brought about in the problem world, is to ensure satisfaction of the requirement. This was essentially the view implicit in my work with Pamela and in my book *Problem Frames* [36], written in 2001. More recently, partly stimulated by many long conversations with Anthony Hall, I have modified my view substantially.

I now see two difficulties with my earlier view. First, many requirements are impossible to formalize. For example, such requirements as 'the system shall be easy to use' or 'the system shall not surprise the driver' defy formalization: people's feelings are not a formal domain, and any attempted formalization is too far from reality to be useful. Experiment can suggest rules of thumb, such as a limit on the number of elements on a screen; and there is room for more specific experiments during system development or in acceptance tests. But experimental results and heuristic rules do not in themselves constitute a formalization. Further, some legitimate requirements may lie outside any reasonable boundary of the problem world. Security requirements may be like this. Attackers may be motivated to exploit physical phenomena and problem domains that lie outside the developers' purview. Power measurement attacks are a notable example, in which measurement of consumed electrical power can reveal information about the computation executed by the machine. Who would have thought it?

The second, complementary, difficulty is that formalization and formal reasoning are essential tools in achieving system dependability. So a highly modified version of Dijkstra's firewall is needed here. Dijkstra's firewall was a formal specification of the desired result of the computation performed by executing the program. (Incidentally, somewhere else he makes the point that the programmer's true product is not the program text, but the computation it evokes when executed.) The equivalent for a cyber-physical system is the problem world behaviour that results from the machine's interaction with the world as it executes the software. So we may regard the problem world behaviour as a firewall between the adequately formalizable problem world and the inadequately formalizable requirements.

D: Does that mean that you regard the requirements as completely non-formal?

J: No. I modify the problem diagram in Figure 9.1 like this:

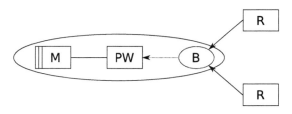

Figure 9.2: An improvement: $M, PW \vdash B$.

The requirements are now understood to be properties of the behaviour—desired and, possibly but not necessarily, formal. The machine and problem world must be adequately formalized, and the behaviour can then be calculated from them. Some requirements may be non-formal; and some may lie outside the problem world. But some, perhaps, may lie inside the problem world and are also adequately formalizable: for these, satisfaction of the requirements can be determined formally from the behaviour B, which itself can be determined formally from the machine specification M and the given properties PW of the problem world. It's always important to stress that the results of the formal reasoning are never more reliable than the fidelity of the formalization itself.

Dijkstra's firewall idea, of course, does not mean that everything beyond the firewall must be informal. It means only that everything within it is formal—or, in systems, adequately formalizable.

D: Did your earlier view cause difficulties in the work you wrote about in the *Problem Frames* book [36]?

J: Not really. The emphasis in the book was on the basic distinction between the machine and the problem world, and between the given properties of the problem world and the properties with which the machine must endow it. The ellipse in the problem diagram of Figure 9.2 represented the requirement only on the assumption that the requirement was adequately formal and lay strictly within the problem world. I think I explained in the preface that wider requirements, lying outside the problem world, were ignored in the book, along with the elicitation and negotiation of requirements. Also, the combination of subproblems into realistic larger problems was treated very sketchily, simply because I didn't understand it at all when I wrote the book. So the deficiencies of my earlier view were, in effect, pushed aside.

D: Does your present view solve these difficulties?

J: I think it goes some way to solving them. I have had a lot of help from Daniel Jackson—my son—and from Anthony Hall, in many extended discussions with each of them. Anthony has been especially insistent in demanding a convincing solution to the problem of combining simple problem frames, and resolutely rejecting inadequate proposals. I think the current idea makes a lot more sense than what I had before.

D: Can you explain it briefly?

J: Yes. The combination of simple subproblems is the combination of simple behaviours. Since simple behaviours are in one-to-one correspondence with the machines of their simple subproblems, their combination is a matter of combining machines.

D: You will probably want to do the formalization of the problem world with more than one formalism, right?

J: Yes. At the very least, the behaviour B of a realistic system is a complex, like a very large concurrent program. And you could have concurrent processes where some of them are dealing with continuous aspects of the world, and some are dealing with discrete aspects. So perhaps you need both differential equations and finite state machines. And this is, of course, only one obvious example of the relevance of distinct formalisms.

D: A quotation that I've encountered in your writings is from John von Neumann's *Theory of Games and Economic Behavior* [47]:

> There is no sense in being precise when you don't know what you are talking about. (cf. [34, p.65])

What are the practical implications of this?

J: What that means to me is that there's a lot of investigation, invention, structuring and design work which must precede any formalization. That doesn't mean that in a big project you have three years of pre-formal work and one year of formal: they must be interleaved in various ways at various levels for various aspects of the development. But one danger in computing is that, just as there is a harmful divide between the academics and the industrialists, so there is a parallel and equally harmful divide between the formalists and the intuitionists. The extreme intuitionists say 'We don't need formalism at all'. The extreme formalists say 'Intuition is mere baseless guesswork: structure must be the product of formal reasoning and calculation'. This conflict has seriously hampered the progress of software engineering.

You need both. The obstacle to combining them fruitfully is clear: too few people are expert and interested in both aspects. I think J. R. Oppenheimer explained how hard it is to get practitioners and theoreticians to work together.

D: So do you see yourself as a practitioner or as a theoretician?

J: Neither, really. I'm more like a gadfly, flitting between both sides and provoking and irritating whichever one I have settled on for the moment.

10. Past, Future, and Adjacent Fields

[During our final tea break:]

J: Do you know about LEO computers?

D: No.

J: The story is amazing. The company J. Lyons & Co. owned a very large catering business. They had teashops all over London, and other larger restaurants. Most of the food they sold was made in their own bakeries. They saw immediately that computers could be useful in business. In 1947 they sent two senior people to Princeton and the University of Pennsylvania to talk to the computer pioneers there. On returning, they financed part of the development of the EDSAC at Cambridge in return for design specifications and some consultancy help. Then they built their own computer— the Lyons Electronic Office. By 1949 they were already trying out a payroll program on the EDSAC. Completion of the LEO computer was delayed by problems with tape drives, but the machine was up and running in 1952, and they had their own data processing system operational in 1953. They took on work for other companies: I think they ran the payroll for the Ford Dagenham factory from 1954.

It was an astounding achievement. They went on and built more computers. After the LEO I, there was LEO II and then there was LEO III. The teashop company had become a computer manufacturer. They developed their own operating system and programming language, and they sold a number of LEO IIs and LEO IIIs. Of course, it couldn't last because LEO computers could hardly compete with companies like IBM. I worked at the LEO computer factory in the summer of 1960. Every day a van appeared with plug-in modules for the computer they were building. The modules were built and supplied by a boat-building firm called Camper & Nicholson: for them, it was a diversification from fitting out luxury yachts. There's a good book [18] about LEO computers. One of the most interesting aspects is the brilliant success of the Lyons data processing systems. The success was largely the result of the attitudes and insight of Lyons operational managers, especially of a man called David Caminer. I think he had great understanding of the relationship between the problem requirements and the possible solutions the computer could help to implement.

LEO I was built 65 years ago: now, only antiquarians of computing are interested. In computing we are very foolish: we don't encourage the study of computing history. It's true that the hardware of a 1950s computer is only of interest to antiquarians. But in development methods, and in the concepts and structures of computer-based systems, we have made too little effort to learn from the past. We have failed not only to learn from the established engineering branches: we have even failed to learn from our own predecessors. I think this failure is due to the compelling attraction of technology—both electronic technology and formal mathematical technology. Some of the most important concerns may seem too philosophical—and may be disdained by some eminent computer scientists for that reason.

D: How might we make more effort to study history? Do you mean just the history of developments like the LEO computer and its systems? Or a broader study?

J: Definitely a broader study. I talked earlier about Vincenti's wonderful book [54] on aeronautical engineering. Anyone concerned with software engineering should read this book. The experiences, the difficulties, and the growth of knowledge in that branch of engineering have much to teach us. But the scope of what we should study extends vertically in time as well as horizontally across engineering branches. In his chapter about the concept of a control volume Vincenti reaches back as far as the early eighteenth century to illuminate the development—and thus the present utility—of the concept. His account is particularly illuminating on the difference between science and engineering, and the reasons why the control-volume concept is vital to engineers but uninteresting to physicists.

There is a compelling analogy here to the gap between formal computer science and practical software engineering. Control volume is a large-scale structural concept, informally instantiated ad hoc for particular applications, which allows engineers to make effective use of physics in analysing their designs. Software engineering needs such concepts. Reading the early work of many computing pioneers, written in the 1970s, 1960s and even the 1950s, reveals a proper and fruitful preoccupation with informal structure. Sadly, that fundamental aspect of software engineering has now largely fallen into neglect.

D: Why is large-scale structure so important? Can it really be effective without a strong emphasis on formalism?

J: One benefit of appropriate large-scale structure is to provide the framework within which formalism can be applied. The control-volume concept provided a framework within which to apply the laws of physics. But structure is of fundamental importance in its own right—it's more important than formalism per se. You need only look at the engineering works of the Romans to see what can be done by informal structural understanding without the benefit even of a good system of arithmetic. They specialized in certain kinds of civil engineering project—roads, bridges, aqueducts, large buildings—and developed a repertoire of structural forms that worked well. The Pont Du Gard at Nimes, the roof of the Pantheon in Rome, and the Aqueduct at Segovia are wonderful achievements.

D: Was this kind of specialization a part of the motivation for your early work on problem frames? And Polya, too?

J: Yes. The solid, repeatable successes of software engineering are the products of specialized disciplines that provide frameworks for dependable design and analysis. Within its limited scope JSP illustrated this point. In a JSP course everyone who understood the method as it was presented would produce the same solution to each of the successive problems. This success, and the comparative lack of success of JSD, stimulated thought about the correspondence between any proposed method and the characteristics of the problems it could address effectively.

Polya explained the notion of the principal parts of a problem, and the ancient Greek distinction between a 'problem to find'— for example, to find a prime between two given primes—and a 'problem to prove'—for example, to prove that a diameter of a circle subtends a right angle at the circumference. It seemed that a method could be defined in terms of the problems it could solve: by the problem's principal parts, their individual characteristics, their relationships, and the solution task itself. This was the genesis [33] of the problem frame idea: the first step in applying a method to a problem is to check that the problem fits the configuration of principal parts that defines the method.

D: Is that where you got the following idea: 'the value of a method is inversely proportional to its generality'? I got that from your 1995 book *Software Requirements & Specifications* [34, p.4].

J: Yes. Writing my earliest thoughts [33] about methods and problem frames I took top-down functional decomposition— also known as stepwise refinement—as one example. When you consider the principal parts of the problems it purports to solve, you see immediately how feeble it is as a method. There is really only one principal part: the function that the machine is to execute. The method is nothing more than recursive decomposition of the function. There are no usable criteria of success, no recognisable difficulties in applying the method, and no identifiable obstacles to its achievement. The problem frame is so general that there is no imaginable problem that cannot be fitted into it. This generality is a disastrous weakness: the method can provide no help with the specific problem because it presumes nothing whatsoever about it. It's reminiscent of Richard Feynman's famous method of solving problems: First, think very hard; then write down the solution. Clearly, a very effective method for Feynman—but very little use to anyone else.

D: What do you think of Stephen Wolfram? Perhaps we won't need every software engineer in industry to be well trained. A couple of institutions of good software developers, such as Wolfram's company (Wolfram Research), might suffice. His company consists of 700 employees and they are building coherent software systems.

I remember you and other panel members discussing in Zurich (2010) whether we will ever get 'good' software engineering in the majority of industries, assuming of course that we all agree on what 'good' means [12].

J: I must admit I know very little about Stephen Wolfram, or about software for mathematical computations. I have read that he has an ambition to make all knowledge computational. I can't imagine how that could make sense. It sounds very like Leibniz's characteristica universalis, intended to reduce all intellectual discourse to a matter of calculation. The ultimate formalization of everything.

I also wonder whether software engineering can be concentrated in a couple of institutions. I think I observed earlier that software is a continuum from a function in an Excel spreadsheet to the software systems in an Airbus. The Internet, and the Internet of Things, seems destined to make the world more and more connected. So it becomes more and more vulnerable to accidental failures and to malicious attacks. If you connect everything together a small mistake in a trivial piece of software can imaginably produce a catastrophe in a connected critical system. Connection is a fine ambition for development. But so also is isolation. Perhaps I'm just revealing my Luddite prejudices here!

[After tea:]

D: Thank you so much for having this conversation with me.

J: You're welcome. I have enjoyed it very much. Thank you for coming to talk to me.

Bibliography

[1] C. Alexander. *The Timeless Way of Building*. Oxford University Press, 1979.

[2] G.D. Bergland. "A Guided Tour of Program Design Methodologies". In: *IEEE Computer* 14.10 (1981).

[3] B.W. Boehm. "Unifying Software Engineering and Systems Engineering". In: *IEEE Computer* 33.3 (2000), pp. 114–116.

[4] B.W. Bowden, ed. *Faster Than Thought: A Symposium on Digital Computing Machines*. London: Sir Isaac Pitman & Sons, Ltd., 1953.

[5] F.P. Brooks Jr. *The Mythical Man-Month*. Addison-Wesley, 1975.

[6] R.M. Burstall and J. Darlington. "A transformation system for developing recursive programs". In: *Journal of the ACM* 24 (1977), pp. 44–67.

[7] J.N. Buxton and B. Randell, eds. *Software engineering techniques*. Report on a Conference Sponsored by the NATO Science Committee Rome, Italy, 1969. Apr. 1970.

[8] J.R. Cameron. *JSP & JSD: The Jackson Approach to Software Development*. 2nd. IEEE Computer Society Press, 1989.

[9] O.-J. Dahl, E.W. Dijkstra, and C.A.R. Hoare. *Structured Programming*. London/New York: Academic Press, 1972.

[10] E.G. Daylight. *Pluralism in Software Engineering: Turing Award Winner Peter Naur Explains*. Heverlee: Lonely Scholar, 2011.

[11] E.G. Daylight. *The Dawn of Software Engineering: from Turing to Dijkstra*. Ed. by K. De Grave. Heverlee: Lonely Scholar, 2012.

[12] E.G. Daylight and S. Nanz, eds. *The Future of Software Engineering: Panel discussions, 22–23 November 2010, ETH Zurich*. Conversations. www.lonelyscholar.com. Heverlee: Lonely Scholar, Oct. 2011.

[13] E.W. Dijkstra. "Go To Statement Considered Harmful". In: *Letters to the Editor, Communications of the ACM* 11 (1968), pp. 147–148.

[14] E.W. Dijkstra. "The structure of the 'THE'-multiprogramming system". In: *Communications of the ACM* 5 (1968), pp. 341–346.

[15] E.W. Dijkstra. *A Discipline of Programming*. Englewood Cliffs, N.J.: Prentice-Hall, 1976.

[16] E.W. Dijkstra. "On the Cruelty of Really Teaching Computer Science, with responses from David Parnas, W.L. Scherlis, M.H. van Emden, J. Cohen, R.W. Hamming, Richard M. Karp and Terry Winograd, and a reply from Dijkstra". In: *Communications of the ACM* 32.12 (1989), pp. 1398–1414.

[17] H.L. Dreyfus. *What Computers Can't Do: The Limits of Artificial Intelligence*. Revised edition (the first edition was in 1972). New York: Harper/Colophon, 1979.

[18] G. Ferry. *A computer called LEO: Lyons Teashops and the Worlds First Office Computer*. Harper, 2004.

[19] J.H. Fetzer. "Program Verification: The Very Idea". In: *Communications of the ACM* 31.9 (1988), pp. 1048–1063.

[20] R.P. Feynman. *Personal observations on the reliability of the Shuttle. Appendix F of the Rogers Report on the Challenger Enquiry*. 1986.

[21] C.A. Gunter, E.L. Gunter, M.A. Jackson, and P. Zave. "A Reference Model for Requirements and Specifications". In: *IEEE Software* 17.3 (2000), pp. 37–43.

[22] P. Brinch Hansen. *The Search for Simplicity: Essays in Parallel Programming*. IEEE Computer Society Press, 1996.

[23] C.A.R. Hoare. "How Did Software Get So Reliable Without Proof?" In: *FME '96: Industrial Benefit and Advances in Formal Methods, Third International Symposium of Formal Methods Europe*. Lecture Notes in Computer Science 1051.

Co-Sponsored by IFIP WG 14.3, Oxford. Springer, Mar. 1996, pp. 1–17.

[24] C.A.R. Hoare. "The Michael Jackson Design Technique: A Study of the Theory with Applications (1977)". In: *Software Requirements and Design: The Work of Michael Jackson*. Ed. by B. Nuseibeh and P. Zave. Introduced by Daniel Jackson. Good Friends Publishing Company, 2010. Chap. 5, pp. 81–113.

[25] C.A.R. Hoare and R.H. Perrott, eds. *Operating Systems Techniques*. A.P.I.C. Studies in Data Processing No. 9. Seminar held at Queen's University, Belfast, 1971. London/New York: Academic Press, 1972.

[26] G.J. Holzmann. "The Model Checker SPIN". In: *IEEE Transactions on Software Engineering - Special issue on formal methods in software practice* 23.5 (1997), pp. 279–295.

[27] D. Jackson. "Alloy: a lightweight object modelling notation". In: *ACM Transactions on Software Engineering Methodology* 11.2 (2002), pp. 256–290.

[28] M. Jackson. *System Development*. Ed. by C.A.R. Hoare. Prentice-Hall, 1983.

[29] M. Jackson and P. Zave. "Distributed Feature Composition: A Virtual Architecture For Telecommunications Services". In: *IEEE Transactions on Software Engineering* 24.10 (1998). Special Issue on Feature Interaction, pp. 831–847.

[30] M.A. Jackson. "The Meaning of Imprecision". In: *Datamation* (1968).

[31] M.A. Jackson. *Principles of Program Design*. Academic Press, 1975.

[32] M.A. Jackson. "Software Manufacture". In: *Computing: The Next Generation*. Ed. by P. Salenicks. Ellis Horwood Ltd, 1988.

[33] M.A. Jackson. "Software Development Method". In: *A Classical Mind: Essays in Honour of C.A.R. Hoare*. Ed. by A.W. Roscoe. Prentice-Hall International, 1994.

[34] M.A. Jackson. *Software Requirements & Specifications: a lexicon of practice, principles and prejudices*. Addison-Wesley, 1995.

[35] M.A. Jackson. "The World and the Machine". In: *ICSE '95 Proceedings of the 17th international conference on Software engineering*. 1995, pp. 283–292.

[36] M.A. Jackson. *Problem Frames: Analyzing and structuring software development problems*. Addison-Wesley, 2001.

[37] M.A. Jackson. "The Name and Nature of Software Engineering". In: *Advances in Software Engineering*. Ed. by E. Borger and A. Cisternino. Vol. LNCS 5316. Springer Verlag, 2008, pp. 1–38.

[38] M.A. Jackson. "Representing structure in a software system design". In: *The Journal of Design Studies, special issue on Studying Professional Software Designers* 31.6 (2010).

[39] M.A. Jackson and P. Zave. "Deriving Specifications from Requirements: an Example". In: *Proceedings of ICSE 95*. ACM, 1995, pp. 15–24.

[40] D.E. Knuth. "Structured Programming with go to Statements". In: *Computing Surveys* 6.4 (Dec. 1974), pp. 261–301. Reprinted with corrections and an addendum as Chapter 2 of [42].

[41] D.E. Knuth. "Literate Programming". In: *The Computer Journal* 27 (1984), pp. 97–111. Reprinted as Chapter 4 of [42].

[42] D.E. Knuth. *Literate Programming*. Vol. 27. CSLI Lecture Notes. Stanford, California: CSLI Publications, 1992.

[43] J.H. Moor. "Three Myths of Computer Science". In: *British Journal for the Philosophy of Science* 29.3 (1978), pp. 213–222.

[44] P. Naur. *Computing: A Human Activity*. New York: ACM Press/Addison-Wesley, 1992.

[45] P. Naur and B. Randell, eds. *Software Engineering*. Report on a Conference sponsored by NATO Science Committee, held in 1968. Jan. 1969. Reprinted in [46].

[46] P. Naur, B. Randell, and J.N. Buxton, eds. *Software Engineering: Concepts and Techniques*. New York: Petrocelli/Carter, 1976.

[47] J. von Neumann and O. Morgenstern. *Theory of games and economic behavior*. Princeton University Press, 1944.

[48] B. Nuseibeh and P. Zave, eds. *Software Requirements and Design: The Work of Michael Jackson*. Good Friends Publishing Company, 2010.

[49] P.F. Palmer. "Structured programming techniques in interruptdriven routines". In: *ICL Technical Journal* 1.3 (1979), pp. 247–264.

[50] D.L. Parnas and P.C. Clements. "A Rational Design Process: How and Why to Fake it". In: *IEEE Transactions on Software Engineering* 12.2 (1986), pp. 251–257.

[51] G. Polya. *How To Solve It*. 2nd ed. Princeton University Press, 1957.

[52] B. Sandén. "Systems Programming with JSP". In: *Studentlitteratur*. AB and Chartwell-Bratt Ltd, 1985.

[53] B.C. Smith. "The Limits of Correctness". In: *ACM SIGCAS Computers and Society* 14,15 (1985), pp. 18–26.

[54] W.G. Vincenti. *What Engineers Know and How They Know It: Analytical Studies from Aeronautical History*. Johns Hopkins University Press, 1990.

[55] N. Wirth. "On the Composition of Well-Structured Programs". In: *Computing Surveys* 6.4 (Dec. 1974), pp. 247–259.

[56] P. Zave. "Classification of research efforts in requirements engineering". In: *ACM Computing Surveys* 29.4 (1997), pp. 315–321.

[57] P. Zave. "'Calls Considered Harmful' and Other Observations: A Tutorial on Telephony". In: *Selected papers on Services and Visualization: Towards User-Friendly Design*. Ed. by T. Margaria, B. Steffen, R. Rückert, and J. Posegga. Vol. 1385. LNCS. Springer, 1998, pp. 2–27.

[58] P. Zave and M.A. Jackson. "Conjunction as Composition". In: *ACM Transactions on Software Engineering Methodology* 2.4 (1993), pp. 379–411.

[59] P. Zave and M.A. Jackson. "Four Dark Corners of Requirements Engineering". In: *ACM Transactions on Software Engineering Methodology* 6.1 (1997), pp. 1–30.

Index

ACE
  Pilot, 8
ACM, 18, 21, 25
Alexander
  Christopher, 42
algebra
  process, 21
ALGOL, 17
American, 9
Artificial Intelligence, 1
assembler, 13, 16
AT&T Research, 4, 69, 73
Australia, 15
Ayr, 5

Baker
  F. Terry, 25
Bell
  Alexander Graham, 7
Bell Telephone Laboratories, 4, 69, 73
Benz
  Karl, 56
Bergland
  Dave, 69
Boehm
  Barry, 62
bomb, 7
Boulter
  Brian, 18, 19
Brinch Hansen
  Per, 30, 31

British, 4, 5, 9, 18, 24, 71
Brooks
  Fred, 54
Broy
  Manfred, 37
Bull Gamma, 11
Burstall
  Rod, 38, 41

C, 20, 69
CACM, 25
Cambridge, 4, 81
Cameron
  John, 4, 60, 69
Caminer
  David, 82
Cantor
  Georg, 8
Civil Service College, 24
COBOL, 13, 16, 18–20
CPU, 28, 32
CSP, 44
cyber-physical, 2, 37, 46, 48, 49, 51, 54, 60, 65, 72, 77

Dahl
  Ole-Johan, 2, 25, 29, 44, 59
Darlington
  John, 38, 41
de Marneffe
  Pierre-Arnoul, 2, 40, 41
Dijkstra

Edsger, 2, 16, 23, 25, 26, 29–
    31, 33, 39, 40, 48, 49, 53,
    55, 59, 62, 65, 77, 78
Dreyfus
    Hubert, 1
Dwyer
    Barry, 2, 4, 15, 16

Edinburgh, 5
Edison
    Thomas Alva, 7
EDSAC, 81
Europe, 7
Event-B, 43
expression
    regular, 20, 22, 66, 67

Fetzer
    James, 1
Feynman
    Richard, 54, 57, 84
flowchart, 15, 66

Gauss
    Carl Friedrich, 50
German, 6
Glasgow, 5
Gloucestershire, 5
grammar, 63

Hall
    Anthony, 75, 76, 79
Harrow, 8
Hayes
    Ian, 37
Hoare
    Tony, 2, 10, 16, 18, 25, 26, 29–
        33, 35, 37, 65, 66
holon, 40, 41
Honeywell, 12–14

Hoskyns
    John, 4, 14–16, 18

IBM, 12, 13, 24–26, 82
IFIP, 4, 18, 29, 70
Imperial College, 4
Infotech, 18, 19, 24, 29

Jackson
    Daniel, 67, 79
Jackson structured programming
        (JSP), 2, 4, 18–20, 22, 24,
        25, 30, 33, 34, 39, 43, 56,
        59, 63, 65–67, 69, 70, 73,
        83
Jackson system development (JSD),
        2, 4, 34, 35, 56, 59, 60, 63,
        69, 84
JCL, 23
Jones
    Cliff, 37

Klein, 8
Knuth
    Donald, 2, 40, 41, 58

Landin
    Peter, 17
Larsen
    Egon, 7
Leibniz
    Gottfried, 85
LEO, 81, 82
Lewin
    Kurt, 35
logic, 1, 10, 32, 62, 64
logician, 47
London, 2, 5, 7, 8, 12, 19, 81

Möbius, 8

Maibaum
    Tom, 35
Manchester, 4, 8
Marconi
    Guglielmo, 7
Mark I, 8
McIlroy
    Doug, 33
Meccano, 6, 7
Merton College, 9, 10
metaphysical, 1
Microsoft, 19
Mills
    Harlan, 25
Misra
    Jay, 37
Moor
    James, 1

NAAFI, 12, 14, 15
National Service, 9, 10
NATO, 15, 16, 24, 33
Naur
    Peter, 1, 2, 32, 48–50, 57, 68
New York, 18, 24
Newcastle, 4, 29
Nimes, 83

Oppenheimer
    J. Robert, 80
OS/360, 23, 54
Oxford, 4, 9, 10, 16

Parnas
    David, 2, 33, 57
Pascal, 58
philosopher, 1
Polya
    George, 35, 83, 84

program
    inversion, 20, 21, 34, 43, 60,
        62, 63, 66

Randell
    Brian, 2, 31, 36
rocket, 7, 40, 41
Rome, 83
Royal Navy, 13
Russian, 10

Salisbury Plain, 12
scheduling, 62, 66
Scotland, 5
Second World War, 5, 6
Segovia, 83
Shanley
    criterion, 40–42
Sintzoff
    Michel, 37
Smith
    Brian Cantwell, 1, 46, 49
Stamp
    Maxwell, 4, 11, 14
Statecharts, 70
Strachey
    Christopher, 2, 5, 8–10
Strathclyde, 4

Teletype, 14
THE, 31, 39, 55

UML, 63
Unix, 20

VDM, 43
Vincenti
    Walter, 35, 68, 82
von Neumann
    John, 79

Watt
    James, 7
Wirth
    Niklaus, 6, 16, 57
Wolfram
    Stephen, 85

Z, 43, 44
Zave
    Pamela, 2, 4, 69–76
Zurich, 85

Also by Edgar G. Daylight:

Conversations

- Pluralism in Software Engineering:
  Turing Award Winner Peter Naur Explains
  2011 · ISBN 9789491386008

- Panel discussions I & II, held at the Future of Software
  Engineering Symposium
  2011 · ISBN 9789491386015

- The Essential Knuth
  2013 · ISBN 9789491386039

- Algorithmic Barriers Falling: P=NP?
  2014 · ISBN 9789491386046

Full-length books

- The Dawn of Software Engineering:
  from Turing to Dijkstra
  2012 · ISBN 9789491386022

Find our latest publications at www.lonelyscholar.com.

LONELY SCHOLAR™
SCIENTIFIC BOOKS

From the same authors:

The Essential Knuth

Abstract

Donald E. Knuth lived two separate lives in the late 1950s. During daylight he ran down the visible and respectable lane of mathematics. During nighttime, he trod the unpaved road of computer programming and compiler writing.

Both roads intersected! — as Knuth discovered while reading Noam Chomsky's book *Syntactic Structures* on his honeymoon in 1961.

> Chomsky's theories fascinated me, because they were mathematical yet they could also be understood with my programmer's intuition. It was very curious because otherwise, as a mathematician, I was doing integrals or maybe was learning about Fermat's number theory, but I wasn't manipulating symbols the way I did when I was writing a compiler. With Chomsky, wow, I was actually doing mathematics and computer science simultaneously.

How, when, and why did mathematics and computing converge for Knuth? To what extent did logic and Turing machines appear on his radar screen?

The early years of convergence ended with the advent of Structured Programming in the late 1960s. How did that affect his later work on TEX? And what did "structure" come to mean to Knuth?

Shedding light on where computer science stands today by investigating Knuth's past — that's what this booklet is about.

www.ingramcontent.com/pod-product-compliance
Lightning Source LLC
LaVergne TN
LVHW022355060326
832902LV00022B/4451